CRi
BANTER

CW00410352

CRICKET BANTER

CHAT, SLEDGING & LAUGHS FROM THE MIDDLE STUMP

DAN WHITING & LIAM KENNA

FOREWORD BY PAUL NIXON

First published 2013
This edition 2014

The History Press
The Mill, Brimscombe Port
Stroud, Gloucestershire, GL5 2QG
www.thehistorypress.co.uk

© Dan Whiting & Liam Kenna, 2013, 2014

The right of Dan Whiting & Liam Kenna to be identified
as the Authors of this work has been asserted in accordance with
the Copyright, Designs and Patents Act 1988.

All rights reserved. No part of this book may be reprinted
or reproduced or utilised in any form or by any electronic,
mechanical or other means, now known or hereafter invented,
including photocopying and recording, or in any information
storage or retrieval system, without the permission in writing
from the Publishers.

British Library Cataloguing in Publication Data.
A catalogue record for this book is available from the British Library.

ISBN 978 0 7509 6001 4

Typesetting and origination by The History Press
Printed in Great Britain

FOREWORD

BY PAUL NIXON

It is a pleasure to write this foreword for Dan and Liam of The Middle Stump, even if Dan does insist on reminding me that his beloved Barnet FC beat my team, Carlisle United, to the Conference title in 2005.

Apparently, I was their first interviewee back in March 2012 when The Middle Stump was just starting out, and since then they have gained a cult following. While *Wisden* they are most certainly not, their particular brand of humour has a place in the game of cricket and I am sure that this book will appeal to the new cricket fan, as well as the more traditional supporter. It was great fun being interviewed and the people in this book that they have spoken to are some of the biggest characters to have played the game in recent years. Let's just say they aren't the usual questions us cricketers get asked!

The articles in this book will keep you laughing all through the season, and the features such as cricketers getting piles, poor behaviour on tour, sledging (for which I was the technical expert!) and getting pinned, will ring true with anyone who has played the game at club or county level! Their article on cricket bats from the 1980s struck a chord with me, as they mention the Gray-Nicolls Scoop, as used by a childhood hero of both mine and Dan Whiting, David Gower. My father bought me a size 3 Scoop when I was a kid, and their look at retro bats brought back many memories.

As for the Guide to Banter section in here, they have even taught me a few new phrases!

The County Guide section will be a great companion to any travelling cricket fan, telling you where to go and grab a pint in a particular town and who's who among the counties, as well as having a laugh at some of the celebrities who hail from that neck of the woods. All in all, a cracking read.

I have played at the ground where they play their local cricket – Southgate in North London, for Leicestershire against Middlesex, and saw Virender Sehwag hit the biggest six I have ever seen in my life. He actually hit the spire of a nearby church. He also put one through the bar window, and the boys from The Middle Stump keep telling me the local glaziers regularly ask 'When is Sehwag coming back?' They also refer to him as Virender the Vandal after that day.

The boys from The Middle Stump are 'old school', like myself, and love having a chat about the game after stumps are drawn, over a beer or three. Cricket needs these people and the larger-than-life characters, like the ones interviewed in this book, are an integral part of why we all love the game.

However, although this book will give you laughs a-plenty, there is also a serious message behind it. A portion of the royalties from sales will go to Factor 50, an excellent charity known to many cricketers. Factor 50 are behind melanoma research, and educating young players to minimalise the risks of skin cancer while they're out in the sun. As cricketers, we are regularly exposed to periods of prolonged sunshine, and the work that these guys do is outstanding. Andy Flower, the England coach is an ambassador for Factor 50, and he ran the London Marathon in 2012 for them as one of his designated charities after having a melanoma removed during the England tour to Australia during the 2010/11 Ashes series. I know they have been into the Durham University Cricket Centre for Excellence, run by ex-England opener Graeme Fowler to educate the students there, and their work should be applauded.

Cricket Banter will make you laugh and it'll be like discussing the game down the pub with your mates. I wish Dan and Liam every success with their book, and look forward to having some of my own banter with them soon.

Nico, 2012

ACKNOWLEDGEMENTS

The boys from the Middle Stump would like to thank the following people who have helped in the making of this book;

DAN: I would like to thank my children: Rebecca; Ben; Hannah; and Beth; a lady who is a little publicity shy but she knows who she is, she encouraged me to write; my mum for her help and support; John Thorp, aka Thorpster, for his contributions to the book and for his banter over the years; Liam Kenna for his chat and helping me write when the going got tough; Gill Nuttall from Factor 50, a dynamo and passionate about her cause; Graeme Fowler who has been brilliant, both with advice and his brand of humour; Paul Nixon who has been a superstar for us and loves good chat; Dan Norcross; Max; Hendo and all the boys and girls at Test Match Sofa; Marcus Charman; Steve James for helping with promotion and for his advice; Tom Huelin and Abby O'Sullivan who helped us write the county guide; The History Press who have answered all of the authors' phone calls and questions with patience and a smile; all the boys at Southgate Adelaide Cricket Club who have taught me a lot – the University of Banter; the supporters of Barnet FC whose humour taught me loads, especially Ruff and Fish, Reckless Tony Hammond for letting me nick one or two of his ideas; Rikki Clarke and the Warwickshire boys for following us and getting involved; Benny Howell and the Gloucestershire boys for doing the same; Steve Beeston Photography, Fred Boycott for helping us to #digin; my uncle George

Berry for teaching me the square cut which I only get out to three or four times a season; everyone who has retweeted us or helped to promote us in any shape or form who we can't all name here but your contribution has been vital; the guys who gave up their time for nothing to be interviewed in this book; and lastly anyone who buys a copy.

LIAM: I would like to thank my dad, Brian, for drumming into me that I can do anything that I put my mind to; my mum, Christell and brothers Justin, Dean and Christopher for spreading the word of The Middle Stump to youngsters around West Wales; Mark Nussey and Adam Fountain; work colleagues who have encouraged me from day one; The Southgate Adelaide boys, who helped make me become the all round good guy that I am today; Gareth Rees and Paul Nixon for getting us off the ground with the first interviews and Gill for getting us access to the stars; the boys at Warwickshire and Glamorgan for their banter and support and of course Foxy Fowler who is, in my opinion, a living legend; everyone who has followed and retweeted on Twitter and to all the Facebook fans; Dan for his secretarial skills, ringing around getting the interviews that we needed, and Thorpy for his essays!

Finally his gran, Eileen, and late grandad, Eddie, who drove Liam all around the country from an early age to play cricket; without their help and support, Liam would have never played the game.

INTRODUCTiON

HOW IT ALL CAME ABOUT . . .

The Middle Stump was started in March 2012 by Dan Whiting and Liam Kenna. Within weeks it had gained cult status among the cricketing cognoscenti as a blog where lad culture met cricket. Followers included Paul Nixon and Gareth Rees initially, and then respected journalists such as Mike Selvey and Steve James.

By July 2012, we had secured a book deal via The History Press and our brand of cricket banter was really out there to a wider public; in changing rooms across the country, county and club cricket teams were all having

a laugh by logging on to our website. Professional cricketers were happy to banter about their teammates via our blog, and soon appearances on Test Match Sofa beckoned. Links with the charity Factor 50 were made, and a donation from the royalties of this book will go to this charity helping fight the battle against skin cancer.

With followers from all around the world among the near 150,000 hits we have had on our website, this book will hopefully give you laughs, fun and frolics as well as helping a worthwhile cause. Interviews with some of the great characters of the cricketing world both past and present, our take on certain aspects of the game and our guide to the first-class counties will give you laughs a plenty, and we hope you enjoy our work.

Dan & Liam, 2012

THE BOYS
BEHiND THE
MiDDLE STUMP

With nearly 150,000 hits on our website and a plethora of Twitter followers, the demand for The Middle Stump is growing by the day.

We are constantly being asked on Twitter who we are, what club do we play for, etc, so here we give you a behind the scenes look at those who write for The Middle Stump.

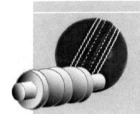

Name: **DAN WHITING**
The Archbishop of Banterbury
Age: 42

CRICKET ROLE

I open the batting for Southgate Adelaide 2nd XI, who play in the Saracens Hertfordshire Cricket League. My bowling has been consigned to the bin, having been the subject of many an insurance policy payout for local homeowners.

NICKNAME

Seve. I was 1st XI captain at my club and not contributing much with the bat. At the time, Mr Ballesteros was the non-playing captain of Europe's Ryder Cup team, and hence the name stuck.

FUNNIEST CRICKETING STORY

Seeing a teammate set himself on fire, having dived after a ball with a packet of Swan Vestas in his pocket comes close, but my favourite was a few years back. I opened and was out for fuck all (as usual), as was our number three. As we walked around the ground debating what to do for the next three hours, we saw a man a good fifty yards away with the reddest face imaginable – he was glowing. My teammate said to me, 'Look at that bloke's face, do you think he likes a beer?' As the said gentleman approached he said in the poshest voice imaginable, 'Excuse me chaps, I don't suppose you know if the bar is open?' We couldn't answer him, we found it so funny.

WORST CRICKETING MOMENT

Having thirty-odd people turn up for a barbecue at cricket for my birthday and getting a golden duck in front of all of my friends.

BEST SLEDGE DELIVERED

While being given a load of gyp by a younger lad all afternoon, I said to him 'Have some respect for your elders. I was in Baghdad, when you were in your Dad's bag', which even made his teammates laugh! He soon kept quiet.

BEST SLEDGE RECEIVED

I was once told an ex-girlfriend of mine (many years ago) was a Ten Pole Tudor of a girl. Apparently she'd had the 'Swords of a Thousand Men'.

FAVOURITE MIDDLE STUMP ARTICLE

Oooh, tough one. I love doing the Q and As – Graeme Fowler, Steve James, Paul Nixon and Mike Selvey were all great – and I enjoyed the Middlesex one too. It has to be said, promoting the Q and As has been great fun and the banter we have had with people like Gill Nuttall from Factor 50 and Graeme Fowler has been brilliant, great fun and helping delivering a message for an extremely worthwhile cause.

EVER PLAYED AGAINST ANYONE DECENT?

I played against Keith Piper and Mark Alleyne for Tottenham a few times when I was a kid. I dropped Alleyne second ball of the match . . . well didn't *drop* him exactly . . . I called for it at the same time as a teammate and then watched it drop in the middle of us. He went on to get 120 not out about two months before he got a contract at Gloucestershire. I played against Phil DeFreitas and Mark Ramprakash, both of whom played at North London cricket clubs.

MOST AMAZING THING SEEN CRICKET-WISE
There is a mate of mine at our cricket club, Matt, who can do a pint in one, upside down while standing on his head up against the dartboard! It's harder than you might think!

BEST TEA
Went to Harpenden once. Frightfully posh. Had king prawns served with garlic. Very nice!

PLANS FOR THE FUTURE
Off to recuperate. I have a bad back from picking up all these names I've dropped! Watch this space, there may well be another Middle Stump book but you never know what is around the corner.

Name: LiAM KENNA
The Sheriff of Banter Town
Age: 24

NICKNAME

Ayrton – for cockney rhyming slang reasons. I have also been called Niki Lauda following an unfortunate incident when I burned my forehead with a hot key.

CRICKETING ROLE

1st XI top-order batsman for Southgate Adelaide CC. Once upon a time I was a leggie until balls started going missing more frequently than an Ian Salisbury full toss. Last season I was loaned out to Datchworth CC – where I drank a lot.

FUNNIEST CRICKETING STORY

I have two that I can't separate. One was away to Old Finchleians and they had an opening batsman who was playing and missing every other ball and then got slapped on the pads in front of all three. As keeper, I went up, as did Dan at first slip and another guy called Flacky, the bowler. It wasn't given. He took ten overs of non-stop stick and abuse from the three of us, which got quite personal at times. He was Chinese and Flacky asked him if he'd had a fortune cookie before the game. This carried on for a while, and we thought he was doing very well to ignore us until their new bat came in and asked, 'Lads, what's the point of sledging this bloke? He's stone deaf!'

My other comes from a man called Corned Beef, my best mate from Wales. He came to stay with me for a summer when I was captaining a game against Winchmore Hill CC. The Beef could bowl more-than-handy inswingers, but had the knack of dropping one short. Hill had James Gatting (son of Mike) opening and boy, he can hit a ball. My only instruction to Beef was to 'not drop it short to Gatting'. First ball Beef steams in and plants one halfway down the track, Gatting obliges and sticks it over the tennis courts onto the main road. As the Beef looks up at the end of his follow-through he mutters, 'Oh fucking hell! Don't tell me that was Gatting? Well I ain't fucking fetching it!'

WORST CRiCKETiNG MOMENT
Dropping two catches in a row in a Test match ground in
Sri Lanka while on tour with London Schools U18s

BEST SLEDGE DELiVERED
Dan will tell you, I'm not much of a sledger. I just talk nonsense.
Fielding at first slip or at short leg, I get up some people's noses
though. Once, while questioning the parentage of a young
batsman after he was dismissed, he turned and put his bat
through the grille of my helmet! My favourite though, has to be
a tag team effort with Dan when Kings Langley's number eleven
needed only a few for the win. We very kindly reminded him that
he could get back page headlines of the *Watford Gazette* and that
Kings Langley needed a hero. Needless to say he soon missed one
and we won.

BEST SLEDGE RECEiVED
Some asshole while playing for Datchworth last year asked me if
my hair was connected to my hat.

FAVOURITE ARTICLE ON THE MIDDLE STUMP

Love how Dan's response was 'Oooh, tough one'. The lunch box wrote his own bloody questions! I like the Foxy one best. Although the Scott Phillips one was great too as it surprised us how many hits it got!

EVER PLAYED AGAINST ANYONE DECENT?

I'm not much of a name-dropper but I've played with and against half of the Glamorgan side (playing club cricket in the South Wales league), as well as some guy in Sri Lanka who got 160 in no time. He was class. Some tosser dropped him twice though.

MOST AMAZING THING SEEN CRICKET-WISE

Matt drinking a pint upside down was amazing. I was also part of ten LBWs in one innings.

PLANS FOR THE FUTURE

Readdress the lbw law. I am an umpire's wet dream.

THE MIDDLE STUMP'S GUIDE TO CRICKET BANTER

Today The Middle Stump gives you the guide to cricket speak. Here are some of the phrases and terms currently being bandied about in cricketing circles. Massive thanks to Thorpster for his contribution to these. If you have any more, please contact us on Twitter @themiddlestump and we would love to hear any more which are doing the rounds. Some of these aren't politically correct, some are long-winded, some are rubbish, but here goes:

ABi TiTMUSS: A sticky dog. Michael Vaughan's debut at Johannesburg could be described as batting on an Abi Titmuss.

AGRiCULTURAL: A batsman known to favour the leg side. *See also* British Airways.

ALiSTAiR CAMPBELL: A spin bowler. *See also* David Busst or Hansie Cronje, but just someone who imparts spin. A lot.

ASSANGE: Named after Wikileaks' Julian Assange, this is a batsman who isn't prepared to accept a decision, one who takes his time at the crease after being given out, or one shocked by an outrageous decision from a lifter, and has to be coerced back to the pavilion by a word or two from the opposition. See Lifter.

AYRTON: A full toss. A delivery which overshoots the track.

BAKERLOO: Playing down the wrong line. As in 'Looked a good ball to me?' 'Nah mate, played down the Bakerloo, when I should have played the Piccadilly.'

BAMBER: Named after Jeremy Bamber, this is someone who is always appealing. Kamran Akmaal is a classic Bamber.

BRITISH AIRWAYS: An agricultural shot played with one's head in the air, as if going plane spotting.

BUNSEN: A wicket that turns square, such as those prepared in the subcontinent virtually every winter especially for England's batting. From Bunsen Burner – Turner.

CHRISTOPHER REEVE: A batsman who refuses to walk, especially after nicking it behind.

DAVID: Rhyming slang for the shower, from the cricketer David Gower. 'I'll be up to the bar in a minute mate, just having a quick David.'

DAVID BUSST: A leg break bowler, named after the ex-Coventry City defender who 'busst' his leg in spectacular fashion in 1996.

DEREK: Rhyming slang for a single, after Derek Pringle. 'Let's be sharp on these Dereks boys!' will often be the cry from the skipper.

DOUGLAS BADER: Short leg.

FERRET: One who goes in after the rabbits. See Rabbit. New Zealand's Brendon Bracewell was a classic ferret.

FiRE OUT: An umpire who lifts his finger very quickly. *See* Lifter.

GC: Meaning (Welwyn) Garden City. When a fielder in close proximity to the batsman cuts off a cheeky Derek, he will get the cry of GC, meaning 'Well in'.

GEORGE BUSH: A premeditated shot/strike/sweep. KP's switch hit is a George Bush.

GRAHAM RiX: An Under 15s game.

HANSiE CRONJE: A wrong 'un. A googly or a chinaman delivery. When a new batsman goes to the wicket he will ask his partner something along the lines of 'What's this bloke like? Just bowling David Bussts?' And he will reply 'Nah mate, he's got a good Hansie.'

JiMMY CARR: A player who doesn't pay his dues/subs/match fees.

JiMMY TARBUCK: A difference of opinion. Ian Botham and Ian Chappell had a Jimmy Tarbuck, as did Mike Brearley and Dennis Lillee over the aluminium bat. Robert Croft and Mark Ilott had one about the light, while Mikey Holding infamously booted down the stumps in New Zealand over the standard of umpiring when John Parker nicked one behind and Christopher Reeved it!

JiMMY WHiTE: A no ball

KATE NASH: Laying the foundations. If on tour, you see a girl in a bar early in the evening (while you're still *compos mentis*), you put in the Kate Nashes – having a sensible conversation before trying to whisk her back to your room in a drunken state at 2.00 a.m. *See also* Mick Hunt.

KiM HUGHES: An umpire who folds easily under pressure. A couple of loud ones from a team of Bambers and this guy will fire out. Named after the Aussie skipper Kim Hughes who broke down in tears in a press conference due to being under pressure.

LEG SIDE LARRY: A batsman who tends to bring his bottom hand into a shot, thus favouring the leg side. Note, although Viv Richards tended to do this, he was no Leg Side Larry. He was just class.

LIFTER: An umpire, normally one who belongs to the opposition, who will give three or four lbws in an innings. Often happy to give a couple of his own tail-enders out as sacrificial lambs in the first innings, he is then happy to fire three out of your top four out in return. Then in the bar, he often will be heard to claim, 'I gave decisions out for both sides ... You can only give what you see,' and other such nonsense.

MANDELSON: 'Go down and field at Peter can you please, mate?' Not to be confused with Sutcliffe or Crouch, this would be to field at third man, after Peter Mandelson's role in the New Labour government, often lurking in the shadows behind Tony Blair and Gordon Brown.

MICK HUNT: In honour of the Lord's groundsman, and very similar to doing a Kate Nash. Doing the groundwork may also apply to the first 20 runs of an innings.

MAX MOSELEY: A swinger. A bowler, often of the Tommy Rundler variety, who swings the ball excessively.

PETER CROUCH: Long leg.

PETER SUTCLIFFE: A batsman known to give it some right hammer.

RABBI: A batsman who will get runs only on a Saturday. See Vicar.

RABBiT: Those who can't bat, often coming in at nine, ten or eleven. *See also* Ferret.

ROD HULL: A batsman who tends to hit the ball in the air a lot, or will go aerial. Named after the ex-Emu puppeteer who tragically died trying to fix his TV aerial.

SHiRT FRONT: A pitch of good quality, completely free from blemishes, and one which a lot of runs should be scored on.

SPECKLES: Almost certainly an urban myth originating from the Kwazulu Natal cricketing fraternity of South Africa. Speckles is a game played with four people or more sitting round a table. One member has to defecate in the middle of the table before retaking his seat. The cricket scorebook is then used to hit said excrement violently, and the person with most speckles on his face has to buy the next round.

STARBUCKS: See Jimmy Carr.

STEPHEN HENDRY: A pitch of poor quality. Named after the acne-affected Scottish snooker player.

TEAMMATE'S MUM: A match situation when the captain needs a good tight spell from his bowlers, or for the fielders to be tight in 'on the Dereks.' Often the shout will go out that, 'We need to be tighter than (pick any teammate's) mum.' Note: Be selective on who you choose for this one, as it can often foster dressing room disharmony.

TiGER WOODS: A player who performs well away from home.

TiTANiC: Name given to a not-so-attractive young lady. While she may look alright in the shady lights of a darkened nightclub, you may find the following morning she has a 'dodgy boat' and isn't as pretty as she seemed the night before after ten pints.

TOMMY RUNDLER: A bowler of low speed, often huffing and puffing his way to the crease. When the shout comes out from the scorer, 'Bowler's name?' and you cannot discern the reply, this man is often entered in the scorebook as 'T. Rundler'.

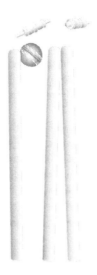

UMPiRE'S WET DREAM : A batsman who is often out lbw. England's batting in the winter of 2010/11 in the subcontinent with the DRS could be described thus. Graham Gooch was also one to Terry Alderman in the 1989 Ashes.

ViCAR: A batsman who will only get runs on a Sunday. The antithesis of a rabbi. Rabbis tend to get their runs, or go to work on Saturdays during league games, whereas a vicar will get his normally against inferior opposition in a friendly on the Sunday.

ViNTCENTS: Numerous cricketers suffer from the dreadful affliction of piles, in this instance named after ex-Middlesex bowler Vintcent van der Bijl.

WESTON: A Super 'Mare. Not just having a bad game, but a shocker. In the bar on a Saturday night the conversation will go like this: 'How did you get on today, mate?' I had a complete Weston. Got a duck, 0–40 off of four overs, and dropped two catches.'

ED GIDDINS INTERVIEW

Ed Giddins has a chequered history. He is among the select band of players to have his name on the board at Lord's for taking five wickets in a Test in 1999, but this was after Giddins had been banned for testing positive for cocaine in 1996.

Here Ed gives us the truth on Eddie Hemmings' high-fashion style, and Norman Gifford removing the chips at Lord's. An interesting and bloody good bloke, he was one of the game's high-profile characters in terms of banter, and we caught up with him as he travelled from Bedford to Cardiff. Ed is now one of the leading poker players in the country and does a great deal of charitable work for the PCA as well as being an after-dinner speaker. Honest and forthright, Ed is fantastic value, as this Q & A session clearly shows.

TMS: Ed, thanks for agreeing to do a Q & A with us. It must be a huge privilege?

EG: I'd never heard of you, but you're the only one that has asked me, so I thought I had better say yes.

TMS: How is retirement? Are you still playing lots of poker?

EG: I hardly play at all these days, apart from maybe a two- or three-hour session online per week. However, I did play in Jimmy Anderson's poker night last night at the Ritz, which was very well attended, for his benefit. Steven Finn played and let me tell you this; his ability with a cricket ball is directly proportional to his inability at poker. He is without a doubt one of the best cricketers but worst poker players I have ever seen. He passed every hand and is the most boring player of all time. If he plays his cricket like that, he will be better than Glenn McGrath as a bowler, because if he is as boring . . . no that is the wrong word . . . as disciplined as Glenn, he'll be a world-beater. He might not trouble the scorers at poker, but I reckon he'll trouble the Aussie top order next year!

TMS: Are you still playing cricket?

EG: I still turn out for Eastbourne on a Saturday and I'm now registering all of late 60s mph with the ball. The keeper stands up and I get the odd wicket on reputation. I come through about as quick as Swanny's quicker ball, I suppose. We are bottom of the league this year, but top when it comes to team spirit!

TMS: Who was the worst dressed you ever played with?

EG: Without a doubt, Eddie Hemmings. He used to wear knitted cardigans from 1948, although he was comfortable with it. He could have modelled for Millets if he'd lost 7 stone.

TMS: Who could drink the most when you played?

EG: Without a shadow, Neil Lenham. He'd have averaged 99.95 if he could bat like he drinks. He just had an extraordinary capacity.

TMS: And the least?

EG: I can't think of a bad one. It's not like these days when they all go for an ice bath, know what I mean?

TMS: Who had the best banter on the circuit?

EG: Nadeem Shahid had great banter. We both bantered around Australia for four years.

TMS: Who threw the worst strops when they were out?

EG: That's an easy one. Mark Ramprakash. A killing machine.

TMS: Who was the worst dancer?

EG: I wouldn't really know, as you know I was always tucked up in bed when the boys went to a nightclub. The best though was Carlos Remy. He danced in a Madonna video back in the late '80s and people would just stop and admire him. He was class.

TMS: What is the best sledge you have received?

EG: Adam Hollioake, after I came back from my ban.

TMS: The first one?

EG: Yeah after my first ban and I was at Warwickshire, I came into bat and before I'd received a ball he said, 'We'd better put in a snort leg!' He must have been thinking that up for ages though because he is Australian and you know what their humour is like … It was a good one though.

TMS: Who was the quickest you have ever faced?

EG: I've turned down singles a few times in my career but the one I have to say was Wasim Akram. He came into bowl at me once and the first time I saw it, no word of a lie, was when the keeper passed the ball to first slip. I just did not see it. I faced Courtney as well but that was towards the end of his career. Wasim definitely stands out.

TMS: What were you taught as a youngster about sun protection?

EG: Sweet FA when we were young. Nothing. Maybe on an a tour there was a bit of sunblock being passed around but apart from that, nothing. I have a pterigyium in the eye from the wind and the sun, and one day I may have to have it removed.

TMS: What do you know about Factor 50?

EG: They do a fantastic job, helped in this day and age by the world of social networking. I applaud them for the great work they do.

TMS: Best food on the circuit?

EG: Lord's. You'd quite happily pay for the standard of food served up there. Before the days of nutritionists they used to serve huge portions of chips. We got bowled out for eighty-odd when I was a youngster and Norman Gifford removed all the chips in a strop. And their rack of lamb was in a different league.

TMS: Best youngsters coming through in England?

EG: James Taylor. When I turn on my TV and Notts are playing I can't wait to watch him. He's exciting and a superstar. Being a small guy, he hasn't got the levers some of the bigger guys have got, but he makes up for it with his timing. Steven Finn is the other one. I think he will be world class. If he carries on there is no reason why he won't get 300 wickets at 24 apiece.

TMS: So Ed, what does the future hold for you?

EG: Well I have my own website which I'd recommend you have a look at – www.edgiddins.com – and I also do a lot for the PCA Benevolent Fund, which is a great cause. I am an after-dinner speaker and I am an auctioneer at a lot of testimonial dinners. I've got a decent style and I raise a few quid for some worthy causes.

TMS: Ed, thanks a million and I really appreciate your honesty. We'll have to have a few beers when we catch up.

EG: Definitely, if I see you around the circuit I'd be more than happy and you're very welcome.

And with that, we left Ed to drive from Bedford to Cardiff and hope he isn't still stuck in Dunstable!

THE THORPSTER GIVES YOU HIS TAKE ON CRICKET TOURS

Whether six months away in Australia, a calypso winter/early spring in the Caribbean or a week on the lash somewhere down on the South Coast, cricket tours have always been synonymous with one thing, and that is bad behaviour.

As an international cricketer steps onto the tarmac about to board the first-class section of a Virgin flight to Kingston, or a club cricketer stumbles out of a bar into the back of his mate's old banger, the phrase 'what goes on tour stays on tour' is guaranteed to be heard ... roughly translated as, 'For God's sake don't tell the missus, whatever happens.'

Freed from the shackles of domestic duty, cricketers are renowned for letting their middle stump guard down and, aided by their preferred tipple, getting into scrapes which would frankly take some explaining if they become public knowledge. While this isn't confined solely to cricketers (just ask Mike Tindall), it seems that those donning the whites have almost monopolised the market.

Now the bad behaviour on tour I am referring to can take place both on and off the field and at any level from the international arena to the annual club mid-season trip. As a young lad aspiring somewhat unrealistically to a profession in the game, I revelled in the red-top headlines of Botham 'allegedly' breaking the bed during an all-nighter with ex-Miss Barbados Lindy Field and a few years before his widely reported Jimmy Tarbuck (difference of opinion) with Ian Chappell in an Australian bar. Moving on a few years, I chuckled while taking in the tales of Tufnell in a toilet cubicle in a New Zealand bar with plumes of 'sweet-smelling smoke' rising over the top of the door, and on another tour his attempt at interior design in an Australian hotel room after a 'difficult' conversation with his then wife. Jumping forward to recent times, Freddie Flintoff's late-night attempt at replicating the Americas Cup in the Caribbean is another incident which has become the stuff of legend.

On the field, Gatt's legendary finger-pointing rant at Shakoor Rana and John Snow's confrontation with a lively and lubricated Aussie fan at the SCG in '71 are two which spring to mind.

My own memories of tour incidents at club level can in some ways be compared to such incidents. There is an allegation that while captain in the West Indies in 1980/81 the aforementioned Beefy banned Mr Gooch from his early morning jogs as he and Gower did not want to be caught returning from their 'nocturnal activities'. Well, a similar thing happened on a club tour to Somerset in 1990. Two club members, not well known to each other and of shall we say differing personalities, were thrust together in a room-sharing arrangement. The younger and more lively half of the partnership had his older more studious occupant described as 'a biker who is a right laugh'. During that tour despite sharing a room for a week, they were never actually inside the room at the same time. The only times their paths crossed was when the older man playing the Gooch role, set off for 5.00 a.m. hikes on Exmoor, and the younger man playing the Beefy role, arrived back, usually not alone, from his night out.

Another tour story about Beefy is that if his skipper came in on the morning of a Test match and said, 'We're batting, lads', Ian, despite often batting at six or seven, would stick his pads up and tell his teammates to wake him up when he was in before proceeding to lie on a bench to sleep off his hangover. In a similar vein, an opening batsman came down to a club tour I was on in Hastings on a Thursday night with the intention of playing a long innings on the Friday at the new county ground. The next morning, and decidedly worse for wear, the opener asked his skipper if he could bat at number three in order to sober up a bit, stuck his pads on and crashed out in his motor for a kip. As the first wicket went down, frantic efforts were made to wake the star batsman up, which continued as the second, third, fourth, fifth and sixth wickets fell. Finally, as wicket number seven went down the 'opener' stuttered into life and after much cajoling was escorted to the crease. After taking about 10 minutes to mark his guard, his innings lasted two balls, both of which he missed by a mile and as the second crashed into his middle stump, he stumbled back to the motor for the last half hour before tea.

I also remember another on-field incident during a game at Worthing, which could be compared to the Gatting v Rana incident. As usual turning up nursing thumping heads, we could just about field eleven players who were alive. In contrast the home side had not only eleven players but an umpire and scorer and also a few spectators. Batting second, as the home side took the field and our two openers made their way to the crease, the host skipper noticed a decided reluctance from our side to make up the second umpire. The skipper, usually a mild-mannered chap, marched onto the pitch and exclaimed, 'You can't expect us to provide a scorer and two umpires throughout the game!' followed by the statement 'THIS IS NO LONGER A FRIENDLY!'

Young tourists are always particularly vulnerable and therefore come in for some 'special treatment'. Such treatment was meted out to a teenage tourist who, on the first night of his virgin tour, became particularly inebriated after consuming many pints of Red Stripe. He was escorted back to the room by concerned fellow tourists and advised to leave his door unlocked in case he required further care. The mob soon returned and as the lad lay snoring, he was quickly covered from head to foot in shaving foam and had a rosebud inserted where the sun doesn't shine for good measure. When he awoke from his Red Stripe-induced slumber he was convinced by the sniggering and his bodily soreness that he had in fact been deflowered and not only by the rose. He soon realised otherwise, but to this day is serenaded by the line 'Now that your rose is in bloom', from the Seal hit, 'Kiss from a Rose'.

There are other legendary tales which have done the rounds of cricket clubs across North London and Hertfordshire that I have had no personal involvement in or corroborating evidence of, but never let the

30

truth get in the way of a good a rumour. The most outrageous is that of a country hotel laying on a particularly warm reception for a side from north-west London. Their visitors made things far warmer, by somehow contriving to burn down one of the rooms they were occupying, leading to the hotel engaging the services of the local fire brigade. Let's just say they weren't welcomed back the next year.

Of course most cricket tours across the country and the world at whatever level go off smoothly and without any incident similar to those outlined above and form an integral part of the cricketing calendar. But if you are inclined to get involved in antics which you would not go near to in everyday life, please remember to agree on the immortal rule for all tourists – 'what goes on tour …'

THE LORD OF LORD'S

Mike Selvey was an outstanding performer back in the 1970s and '80s. His record of bowling in one-day finals was second to none, and here, the ex-Middlesex, Surrey, Glamorgan and England bowler, now chief cricket correspondent for the *Guardian*, talks to The Middle Stump about those heady days at Middlesex, and with England. He still holds the record for most Middlesex wickets in a county season. A man with a keen interest in beer, guitars and golf, Selve talks us through bowling at Viv, the cakes at Worcester and answers various other questions, Middle Stump style.

> **TMS**: Mike, thanks for agreeing to do a Q & A with The Middle Stump. It must be a huge privilege for the cricket correspondent of a highly respected broadsheet, such as the *Guardian*, to be associated with The Middle Stump?

> **MS**: It's a dream come true.

> **TMS**: What do you think of our work so far?

> **MS**: Coming along nicely. The more the merrier, too. I like the online growth of interest in cricket, particularly the global aspect of it.

TMS: Let's start with your playing days, and most people associate you with Middlesex but you moved from Surrey a few years before, didn't you? It takes a brave cricketer to cross the Thames. No Ramprakash-style witch-hunts back in those days?

MS: I don't think they noticed I was gone until we played them. Essentially though they said there was no room there, although if I'd told them I knew Bob Willis was moving, they might have thought otherwise. Who knows? But I was born in Middlesex. And I never liked the atmosphere at The Oval.

TMS: Those Middlesex days in the '70s must have been good times?

MS: Just the best. We developed into a really good team, although we never really came to terms with the shorter forms as we ought. The longer the game, the better we were. We don't catch up often but the winter before last we had a lunch at Lord's and just spent hours in the dressing room afterwards with a case of red. During the World T20 in the Caribbean, I met up with Wayne Daniel, who lives in Barbados, and Vince van der Bijl and it was the first time we had been together since 1980. A magic evening.

TMS: Who liked a beer the most out of that side? Anyone in the league of Frank Hayes at Lancashire who we understand used to have sixteen pints a night?

MS: I think that might be me. But nothing like Frank Fish, though sixteen a night I suspect is hyperbole (that would have represented a swift half for Ollie Milburn mind you). Incidentally, Fish was just the strongest man. Stronger than Pete Willey .... stronger than Beefy.

TMS: Do you think the social side of cricket is disappearing with players not so inclined to have a beer together at the end of play?

MS: Definitely, in the context you suggest. I learned a lot from talking to opposition players and I still think it could be important to do that. Always take time out to pick the brains of good players. Even if mostly you don't find anything to incorporate into your own game, sometimes you unearth a gem.

TMS: You liked a Gillette Cup final, taking 2–17 and 2–22 off of your 12 overs in 1977 and 1980. What were those occasions like to play in?

MS: I bowled in four finals – three Gillette and one B&H – 47 overs in all and never went for 100 runs in total. We played all of our home cricket at Lord's, so the ground itself held no great mystique. But it was great to have a sell-out crowd. The 2-17 in 1980 included a six, so basically I bowled 11.5 for 11, or a minimum 60 dot balls.

TMS: You took 101 wickets in 1978, which no Middlesex bowler has achieved since. Do you think anyone will do it again? Murtagh came close last year, didn't he?

MS: Didn't Embers take 100 in 1984? You need to bowl a lot of overs to do so, which is not so easy with sixteen County Championship games. Perhaps you get nineteen matches top whack. I think I bowled around 750 overs for that.

TMS: In 1976 you played for England against the mighty West Indies and started brilliantly, taking 3–6 off of your first twenty deliveries. Did the thought of Test cricket being a piece of piss ever cross your mind?

MS: At that point I think I had the best career strike rate of any Test bowler in history, who had taken three wickets. It might even be the case today! I peaked too early, you see.

TMS: Was there a time bowling at Viv during his 291 at The Oval that you didn't know where to bowl?

MS: Not really. But it was seriously flat, he was seriously relentless, and never looked like getting out until, unaccountably, he did. Every pace bowler in the match struggled for wickets apart from Mikey Holding, who just made a mockery with what I still think is the greatest display of fast bowling ever.

TMS: Any batsmen ever made you feel like that?

MS: John Steele of Leicestershire.

TMS: Who was the quickest bowler that you ever faced?

MS: Mikey. I got a rousing round of applause for straight driving my first ball in Test cricket back past him for two. Truth is it just hit the bat and ricocheted back past him. Fastest single delivery I ever saw live was Shoaib Akhtar to Stephen Fleming in the 1999 World Cup semi at Old Trafford. Forget that alleged 100mph thing in South Africa. That was my pace.

TMS: Do you miss playing or do you prefer journalism?

MS: It's been good to remain in touch with the game. I do still get the odd pang. During the winter, I was watching my young son in some indoor nets, and just hanging around with a ball in my hand. So I thought I might turn my arm over and then got increasingly enthusiastic until I ended up tear-arsing in to this quite decent seventeen year old. Nabbed a three-for but then he dilscooped me and that was the end of that. I am 64 though.

TMS: Were you taught anything about the dangers of being exposed to the sun for prolonged periods of time when you played?

MS: Not really and it is something that was so wrong. When we went on holiday in those days you actually put oil on to cook you, not protect. I don't recall ever putting sun protection on other than a hat.

TMS: What do you think of Factor 50 and the work that they do via cricket?

MS: I think it is brilliant. I was in Australia when Andy Flower had his melanoma removed and know how lucky he felt that it had been spotted when it was. I hope his recent marathon helped raise the profile of an organisation doing important work.

TMS: Best teas on the circuit? I know both you and Graeme Fowler are fans of the cake in the Ladies Pavilion at Worcester!

MS: The lemon sponge cake in the Ladies Pavilion at New Road is just from another planet. And so is the price: £1 a slice. It would be churlish not to, wouldn't it?

TMS: What does the future hold for you?

MS: Churning out the words for as long as I have kids to educate. I can't see the light at the end of the tunnel just yet. But then who wants to retire? I still enjoy the companionship of cricketers and cricket people.

Mike, we don't want to see you retire just yet either, and it was great to have a chat with a genuine cricket person. You can follow Mike on Twitter @selvecricket and for those who love their cricket, it's worthwhile.

BAT TO THE FUTURE

The Middle Stump's guest blogger, the Thorpster, gives us a hilarious insight into what bats were like in years gone by, and a few differing uses for them as well. If you have ever used a Double Scoop, Powerspot, SS Jumbo, Slazenger V12 or even a St Peter, then read on, and I'm sure it won't be long before you're nodding your head in appreciation.

While reading an article in *The Times* about the now infamous Anders Breivik, I was intrigued to learn that he had nicknamed his gun Mjolnir. Apparently this was after Thor's hammer, not the '90s cricket bat by John Newbery, also named after the mythical tool. I then began thinking about the bats I owned over the years and how the weapon of choice for batsman has changed since I started playing cricket in the early '80s.

In those days choice was limited to mainly bats made by Gray-Nicolls, Gunn & Moore, Stuart Surridge, Slazenger and Duncan Fearnley. The choice was normally made dependent on who, as a budding cricketer, you associated yourself with. For the classy stroke player likening himself to David Gower or Greg Chappell it was Gray-Nicolls, and probably the Double Scoop. The problem with the Scoop was that frankly, there was more wood on a drumstick and more meat on a jockey's whip, and not many of us time it like Gower, so unless you absolutely middled it, hitting boundaries was never easy. I personally began with a Gray-Nicolls World Cup, which had a middle the size of a pea, and I think at one time was utilised by the dazzling Chris Tavare!

Another stroke player's favourite was a Gunn & Moore bat, as initially used by Mike Gatting. At one time I had a Striker by GM and when facing a quick, the vibrations often shot through the body on impact. Boycs used a Slazenger at that time, and prior to the more meaty V12, their bats were thought of more for the caress through the covers than the wallop over mid-wicket.

For the more explosive type of player it was usually either the SS Jumbo (as used at times by Viv Richards and Graham Gooch), or a Duncan Fearnley, usually a Magnum, also wielded by the aforementioned pair from time to time. Duncan Fearnley also produced the Attack by Ian Botham but there was much debate at cricket clubs across the land as to whether Beefy, the darling of the masses, *really* utilised a £30 bat to despatch bowlers to all parts?

As time moved on, so did the choice of brand available and Gatt moved on to the first Newbery bat, with garish and infamous orange and black stickers. Strangely, at the end of the handle was a metal counterbalance which in my experience was prone to falling out at inopportune moments. Maybe that was what Gatt was searching for in the grass verge at the Rothley Court Hotel in the incident leading to the termination of his England captaincy?

Newbery bats soon became very popular, basically because even a thick edge would go for four and they developed further bats such as the Series One and the Mjolnir. At my club, Southgate Adelaide CC, the bats were very popular, particularly as a discount was available via one of the club's members.

At the end of the 1990s I settled on a Slazenger V100, which was fairly cheap, went quite well and was also fairly durable and therefore economic. Jumping forward to today and any number of brands are available that were unheard of in terms of cricket bats in the '80s. Kookaburra, Woodworm and other sports brands not associated previously with cricket such as Puma, Adidas and Reebok bats are on show at every level of the game. Also many brands have come from India, along with specialist bats such as the Mongoose, used for big hitting in the shorter versions of the game.

Some of the greatest batsmen of yesteryear also had other factors to consider when making their choice of blade. In the case of Javed Miandad, the infamous 'street fighter', he had to consider which bat to use when whacking Dennis Lillee, eventually opting for the Gray-Nicolls Powerspot, whereas in choosing a bat to attack some inebriated Canadian 'cricket fans' in a Sahara Cup match in 1997, Inzamam opted for a CA.

Maybe the most popular alternative use of the willow, which goes on every week across the country in club cricket, is to smash one's own stumps down in frustration at being dismissed. The most famous incident of which was Chris Broad at Sydney in 1988 after being bowled, despite having scored a hundred in the Bicentennial Test, utilising one of the original railway sleepers, the Duncan Fearnley Magnum.

Whatever cricket bat you buy for this season, you can guarantee that they are better than the willow we used back in the '80s, and bat manufacturing has come on a long way.

THE MIDDLE STUMP MEETS STEVE JAMES

The Middle Stump have waxed lyrical about our favourite thought-provoking journalist, Steve James, recently. So it was an absolute privilege for us to speak with him about his new book *The Plan*, quick bowling and our usual banter, although Glamorgan skipper Mark Wallace might not think so. Read below as we catch up with the ex-Glamorgan and England opener.

TMS: Steve, thanks for agreeing to do a Q & A with The Middle Stump. As a cricket correspondent with a respected broadsheet it must be a privilege to appear in such a classy publication?

SJ: Ha! I'm only the cricket columnist at the *Sunday Telegraph*, mind. Scyld Berry is correspondent. Maybe one day …

TMS: What do you think of The Middle Stump so far?

SJ: Very good!

TMS: Do you prefer being a journo or playing? Do you miss playing? Do you still play club cricket? And do you prefer writing on rugby or cricket?

SJ: I don't miss the pressure and worry of playing, but I do miss the thrill of scoring a century, and playing touch rugby with the lads in the morning ... I've played a few games (not for five years after I finished with a knee injury though), but I can't say I've particularly enjoyed them! I prefer writing on rugby obviously – it doesn't take as long! I love both, of course.

TMS: What is the book *The Plan* about?

SJ: It's about England's journey from being bottom of the rankings in 1999 to top in 2011, looking especially at the influences of Duncan Fletcher and Andy Flower, two people I know very well. It's about a lot besides though, central contracts, the academy, Peter Moores, etc.

TMS: How is it different from your previous book, *Third Man to Fatty's Leg?*

SJ: It's not all about me! Although there are plenty of personal memories.

TMS: What the bloody hell went down at Glamorgan last year?

SJ: Professional cricket shouldn't be played in early April. Pitches have been spicy. Glam were missing James Harris badly. Nobody is getting runs but sides would be getting a lot fewer if he was playing.

TMS: Having held the record with a cheeky little 309 for Glam, could you still do a job at the top of the order?

SJ: No chance.

TMS: Who was the quickest you ever faced and were you ever bricking it as they were coming in to bowl?

SJ: All batsmen are scared. That thing hurts! Rudi Bryson in Pretoria in 1996. Scary ...

TMS: Who was the maddest you played with and against?

SJ: David Hemp.

TMS: Best sledge received?

SJ: Graeme Fowler thought I looked like Chris de Burgh so he always used to sing 'Lady in Red' as I walked out to bat. Sledging is so overrated. It's mainly abuse.

TMS: Who could drink the most and the least in your experience on the circuit?

SJ: Most: Matthew Maynard. Least: Mark Wallace.

TMS: Which of your teammates could handle a vindaloo and who would wimp out and have a korma?

SJ: Same as above. Wally actually struggles with a korma! We have a curry club that meets regularly including him, Gareth Rees, Mike Powell, Ian Thomas, my benefit chairman Ian Williams, Gwyn Jones, Ian Bird and some others.

TMS: Best teas on the circuit?

SJ: Abergavenny.

TMS: Ever played at our ground, Southgate in North London, and if so, what are your views?

SJ: Yes, it was a controversial match where Middlesex were docked points and then had them reinstated. Justin Langer behaved like a pork chop!

TMS: What were you taught about sun protection when you played?

SJ: Not much, sadly.

TMS: What do you think of charities such as Factor 50 promoting skin cancer awareness via cricket?

SJ: Brilliant. Obviously Andy Flower is a great mate of mine and his lucky escape should be an example to us all.

TMS: You opened with Athers at Cambridge didn't you? Does it sadden you to see the universities getting rolled over regularly?

SJ: Athers actually batted at three! We weren't always great either. Universities shouldn't be first class but the system must stay. You should be able to get a proper education and pursue a cricket career.

TMS: Best three youngsters coming through in England?

SJ: Daniel Bell-Drummond, Jos Buttler and Tymal Mills.

TMS: You played rugby at a decent level as well. Do you think the days of dual sportsmen such as Chris Balderstone, Phil Neale, Alistair Hignell, etc are over?

SJ: Yes, no chance sadly. It's difficult enough to keep it going at schoolboy level.

TMS: What do the next few months hold for you? I should imagine you'll be busy with the book won't you?

SJ: Bit of publicity stuff for that, lots of *Telegraph* work, and I'm hopefully starting on a new book with a rugby player ... will keep you posted!

Steve, you were an absolute pleasure to speak to. Best of luck and look forward to speaking soon.

THE FANTASTIC MR FOX

Not many of us get the chance to have a chat with one of our heroes. As a thirteen year old watching the 1983 Cricket World Cup, probably the finest one ever, especially according to The Middle Stump's growing legion of fans in India, I watched as Graeme Fowler – a man whose hairdo at the time made him look like he should have been in Spandau Ballet – hit four consecutive fifties, as England marched on to the semi-finals. Fowler averaged 72 in that tournament.

So when I got the chance to have a chat with him recently, I was thrilled, slightly nervous and wondering what was he really like? After thirty seconds I realised he was one of us. After thirty minutes I was in tears, pissing myself laughing at one of the funniest people I have ever spoken to. The game is poorer for the retirement of characters like Graeme, and although I couldn't remember everything he said, here is what I remember writing, through tears of laughter.

TMS: Graeme, thanks for agreeing to do a Q & A with The Middle Stump.

GF: A pleasure. Obviously it is an ambition fulfilled!

TMS: What do you think of the blog so far?

GF: I've enjoyed what I've read, although it takes me longer to read than most people.

TMS: Do you prefer being running the academy or playing? Do you miss playing? Do you still play club cricket?

GF: I retired in 1994, and played two games in 1995 and that's been it. I loved playing but I knew when I started, that I'd have to finish one day. Now, with the University of Durham Centre of Excellence, I love what I do, absolutely love it. I designed it back in 1996, and it is absolutely fantastic. Besides, I'm unemployable!

TMS: How good was Lancashire winning the Championship in 2011? Envious?

GF: Not at all envious. I think it is fantastic. We came runners up in '87, but cocked it up on the last day, and when they woke up on the last day in 2011, they didn't know if they would win it, so I am absolutely thrilled to bits for them.

TMS: Not many people scored a ton against the 1984 Windies. Who was the best of their bowlers?

GF: Impossible to say. You couldn't split Garner, Holding or Marshall. Then you had Baptiste, who was decent as well. He was no mug. Your eyes lit up when Roger Harper came on to bowl.

TMS: But he could field, couldn't he?

GF: Oh yes, you didn't hit it anywhere near him!

TMS: What was more of an achievement in your book – a ton against them or a double hundred in India?

GF: I can't separate the two things. As an opener, yes, you should get hundreds against a pace attack but then India was mainly a spin attack, so I just enjoyed the knowledge I had the ability to get runs against both. Saying that, I was far from being the complete player!

TMS: Why are you called the Fox? Do you enjoy being chased around by a pack of hounds?

GF: In my first Test at Headingley, Bob Willis introduced me to the team as Foxy Fowler. All day in the field I would chase it, and get a 'Well done, Foxy!' and I thought, 'Who the hell are they talking to?' The name has just stuck. Bob now calls me Graeme, ironically.

TMS: Who was the maddest you played with and against?

GF: Ooooh, good question. With, would have to be Derek Randall, he really was nuts. Against, I couldn't say.

TMS: What about David Smith at Surrey? He was a nutter, wasn't he?

GF: No, I got on well with him. He was 6ft 3in and hard as nails, and I'm 5ft 9in and not. I used to say to him, 'What are you looking at?' in a jokey fashion and we always had a laugh about it.

TMS: Best sledge received?

GF: Not received but it came from Geoff Lawson, who I played with at Lancashire 2nds when he was playing in the Lancashire Leagues, along with me. He was known as Henry, after that well-known Aussie poet, Henry Lawson, who no one has ever heard of. Anyway, we ended up playing a Test against each other, and I was playing and missing a hell of a lot – really out of form – and he was effing and blinding at me. All I could say was, 'Henry, just bowl a straight one.' Anyway, next match I am batting with Chris Tavare, and he has scored about 3 in an hour, and he pushed forward and blocked one into the covers, and called 'Waiting!' Henry piped up with, 'Mate, we're always waiting!'

TMS: And Steve James tells us you always sang 'Lady in Red' when he came out to bat?

GF: True. Guilty. But he does look like Chris de Burgh though, doesn't he?

TMS: Who could drink the most and the least in your experience on the circuit?

GF: The most was Beefy, without a doubt. At Lancashire it was Frank Hayes. He'd have about sixteen pints every night. But I have never seen anyone put it away like Botham. The least, dunno, they never bothered coming out with us!

TMS: Which of your teammates could handle a vindaloo and who would wimp out and have a korma?

GF: Ian Austin for the vindaloo, and whoever wimped out and had a korma, he'd eat theirs too! Jack Simmons could eat though. He once ate four lots of fish and chips. I gave him a lift home once, because he lived near me, and asked me to stop off at the fish and chip shop. He loved his fish and chips, Jack. I've started the car and he's gone 'Where in the bloody hell do you think you're going?' I said, 'Dropping you off home!' and Jack said 'Don't do that, or the wife won't make me any tea when I get in.' He made me sit there in my car while he finished his fish and chips.

TMS: Who was the quickest bowler you ever faced?

GF: Jeff Thomson. By miles and miles.

TMS: Best teas on the circuit?

GF: Lord's – always been good. Worcester used to have great cakes in the Ladies Pavilion, served by women with proper pinnies on. In my current role, it has to be Usk CC in Wales – fantastic teas.

TMS: Ever played at our ground, Southgate in North London, and if so, what are your views?

GF: Never played there but went there in the universities final and we were playing Loughborough where Graham Dilley was in charge, and it's lovely. Dill was sitting there all day under a tree. An umpire was firing out our lads, and after the fourth one, Dill apologised to me for the umpire ruining the game. Anyway, we wrote a letter to whoever you write to, complaining about the umpire, and it only went to the same umpire who had to sit and adjudge whether he was fit to stand for the following season!

TMS: What were you taught about sun protection when you played?

GF: When I was a lad, and we went to the beach, my mum used to make a mixture of olive oil and vinegar to smother us kids with. It was like this sort of salad cream, so it was no wonder that we had dogs chasing us all day! However, I wasn't really taught anything about it until I went and played in Australia, and then I saw people who had had melanomas removed. Frightening.

TMS: What do you think of charities such as Factor 50 promoting skin cancer awareness via cricket?

GF: They do an unbelievable job. We've had them giving talks to our lads here at Durham about it, you know, educating the students. It should be on the school curriculum, because it is incurable, it leaves huge scars and they send out a big message. One of our lads at Durham is a ginger kid, and he has been out to India for two weeks. He looks like he has been in a cupboard. He got the message and slapped on Factor 50, but it should go out to all youngsters, not just ginger kids!

TMS: Does it sadden you to see the universities getting rolled over regularly? And do you think they should have first-class status? I saw on Twitter recently you were gutted after Durham Uni were bowled out for 18 against Durham?

GF: Yeah I was. The system works; 25 per cent of county players have come through the British universities system. You can debate as long as you want whether we should have first-class status though. The youngsters have to go through a learning process, and if that is getting rolled, then so be it. However, with regards to first-class status, Rob White at Northants told me he concentrates a bit more against the students, as no one wants a duck against them, or in a first-class game, so if that makes things more intense that can only be a good thing. However you can debate all day whether the students should have first-class status.

TMS: Best three youngsters coming through in England?

GF: Ooooh, couldn't really say. I tend to just concentrate on my lads, as opposed to others. Freddie van den Bergh, who is contracted to Surrey, a slow left-armer and Chris Jones, who is with Somerset, both have bright futures ahead of them.

TMS: What do the next few months hold for you?

GF: Well, I'll have less hair. I will lose students who I have worked with for three years, and gain a load of students I know nothing about, and that's about it.

TMS: Graeme, you have been an absolute pleasure to speak with and it's been a good laugh.

GF: And you, and best of luck with The Middle Stump.

And with that, he told me he was off to polish off a bottle of Faustino VII Rioja he had been given recently. When I told him that I also like a Rioja, but prefer Campo Viejo, he replied 'He was one helluva full back'. Laughing to the end, it was a privilege and pleasure to speak with one of the great characters of English cricket.

CRICKETERS AND PILES

Plymouth Argyles, Duke of Argylls, Vintcent van der Bijls, nautical miles, Graham Miles, Nobby Stiles, John Steinbecks (the Grapes of Wrath), Emma Freuds ... whatever cricketers call haemorrhoids, they definitely aren't a laughing matter for those suffering with them. Going into work on a Monday looking like you have spent a weekend at a Michael Barrymore pool party is no fun either!

For some reason cricketers and piles are closely linked. A connection between being on your feet all day standing around, and then exertions such as sprinting, is going to get the grapes dangling. Wicketkeepers and fighter pilots are the two groups which suffer the most according to our sources, and any profession which tries to suck your body through your arsehole is going to make you suffer.

Viv Richards was one of the most well-known sufferers in the modern-day game, actually missing a County Championship game through being unable to walk. It can actually make you quite ill with the amount of blood lost, and has been described as the equivalent of donating a pint of blood. I'm sure the NHS have their own preferred method of donating though, don't they?

An opening bat at our cricket club who eventually had his removed privately by laser, would be known to wear a sanitary towel so as not to dirty his whites, when they were, in his own words, 'producing more claret than a Bordeaux vineyard'.

Ex-England opening batsman Graeme Fowler described Clive Lloyd once in a match as coming down the wicket to him in mid-over. Thinking he had something important to say about the bowler, or maybe to pass on some technical knowledge or advice, Foxy wandered down to meet him mid-track before the big Guyanan just muttered, 'My piles are killing me' before returning to the non-striker's end, leaving the Lancastrian standing there in the middle, absolutely dumbfounded and in a state of shock.

Fowler was no stranger to the surgeon himself when it came to his own grapes of wrath, and was extremely nervous before visiting a physician once in the North-East. When he met the consultant, he saw he had hands 'bigger than Alec Bedser' and he knew what was coming. Not only big, they were apparently extremely bony as well, and not being in his most glamorous position with someone's fingers knuckle deep in his anus, the Lancastrian had a rather surreal conversation with him about opening the batting! He describes it as one of the least dignified experiences of his life.

Godfrey Evans was another cricketer who suffered, as was Ian Botham, although Fowler admits it wasn't the first topic of conversation you would have with people when you saw them around the circuit. Cricketers no doubt will suffer for many more years to come from the unspoken *bête noir*, or should that be *bête rouge*, of the summer season.

Right, where's my Preparation H?

THE PAUL NIXON INTERVIEW

The Middle Stump is attracting a lot of attention via Twitter and one of our followers is former England, Kent and Leicestershire wicketkeeper/batsman, Paul Nixon.

Recently retired, Nico gives us the lowdown on the county circuit, and the game will definitely be poorer without characters like him. Nico tells us about birds, booze and fashion in this hilarious interview, and there were similar stories aplenty in his book, *Keeping Quiet,* which hit the shelves in July 2012 – a must-read for any cricket fan! This is the best Nixon interview since David Frost got his own scoop in the '70s.

TMS: When you played for England apparently you ran around shouting 'I'm living the dream!' Is being our interviewee at The Middle Stump living the dream as well?

PN: I wouldn't exactly say running around shouting it! I may have whispered it here and there. The Middle Stump is obviously a huge honour for me, as it is such a classy set-up.

TMS: How are you coping with retirement after twenty-three years in first-class cricket? Are you playing club cricket? Fancy a game this summer for Southgate Adelaide 2nd XI?

PN: Coping well so far thanks! I'm only playing benefit games as well as Masters Cricket for the PCA … if I played any more cricket I think the wife would divorce me!

TMS: They say a good wicketkeeper is like a good woman – the best ones stay down longer. Any advice for up and coming keepers?

PN: Interesting similarity! My advice would be come up before the ball bounces but only to knee/shin height with your hands, and expect every ball to be edged to first slip's inside foot so that you are in a position to catch it. Then it's not a shock when it's edged.

TMS: Which fellow player pulled the worst bird in your experience in the county game?

PN: While in an SAS pre-season camp we had to catch a chicken, kill it and eat it. Dave Fulton (ex-Kent) pulled its neck and when we opened it up it had cancer, so it has to be Dave Fulton. It was a shocking bird.

TMS: What was your best experience in the game?

PN: Playing in Australia for England – awesome! Close to 90,000 at the MCG.

TMS: You seem to be the king of T20 cricket. What were the reasons behind Leicestershire's success?

PN: We planned well and made sure we put the right people in the correct places and we had very good players.

TMS: Who can drink the most in the county game? And who can drink the least?

PN: Years ago people drank much more; now the game is so much more intense and you can't drink as games take place every other day. Freddie takes some beating! Russell Cobb, ex-Leicestershire, could take two drinks and then he was finished!

TMS: Who is the best- and the worst-dressed player you have shared a dressing room with?

PN: Worst-dressed was Alan Mullally, ex-Leicestershire CCC as he was brought up in Australia, and best-dressed was Mark Ealham, who is Mr Label.

TMS: Where does your nickname of Badger come from? Is it because nasty people build traps at each end of your house, before sending Jack Russells down each end to simultaneously attack you?

PN: Haha very good. It's because of my nocturnal activities.

TMS: What was it like making your England debut at thirty-five, or was it thirty-six? Surely you thought your chance had gone?

PN: I was thirty-six. Yeah, amazing! Any chance I thought I had, had gone in 1995 when Allan Donald snapped my thumb on 51, my first game of the year, while playing for England A.

TMS: The West Indies World Cup must have been difficult for all concerned with the death of Bob Woolmer and the Fredalo incident? What was that like? I thought you had quite a good tournament.

PN: Hearing the tragic news of Bob was shocking – a great man who we have all had some help or advice from. Fredalo cost me £1,500 for a quiet night! Wished I'd gone big for that price, just because I went to bed after midnight! There was no curfew … Freddie was out of the game.

TMS: What is your view of sides playing in March like they do these days? Surely it is still snowing in Carlisle at that time of year?

PN: It's sunny every day in Cumbria! Yep, March is far too early but the ECB want to get Champions League in and IPL in as well as the county season.

TMS: Who are the best wicketkeepers coming through at present?

PN: Michael Bates from Hampshire is a quality wicketkeeper, but nowadays you have to be able to bat.

TMS: How do you view county cricket and is the future T20?

PN: Probably three leagues of six teams, with lots of T20 and 50- or 40-over games.

TMS: Michael Vaughan describes his early days at Yorkshire as being akin to a stag do, play the game and then on it in the evening. Do you think the social side has gone from cricket? I think personally it has at club level. Most teams have one beer before going on their way.

PN: Vaughany is right, we had a ball years ago, but now there is much more money in the game and more at stake, so sadly you can't go big in the evenings.

TMS: He also describes playing the odd Sunday League game hung-over. Ever played with a hangover?

PN: Any player who has played for years has played with a hangover … hic!

TMS: You were one of the great characters of the game and maybe one of a dying breed. Who else is a great character in county cricket?

PN: The funniest man in county cricket is Anthony 'Maggs' McGrath. A great man.

TMS: Best sledge you have dished out/received? Or is it just banter you come out with?

PN: I told Nasser Hussain he was the ugliest and most hated man in county cricket. Not really a sledge, just the truth!

TMS: Favourite ground played at?

PN: As far as England is concerned it's Lord's. Sydney's my favourite abroad.

TMS: Have you ever played at our home ground, the Walker Ground at Southgate, where Middlesex play? And if so, thoughts?

PN: Yes I have a few times … Sehwag hit the biggest six I have ever seen off of Jamie Dalrymple, which hit the church. Needs changing rooms the same level as the tea rooms but an OK ground. Very slow pitch!

TMS: Tea is one of the most important aspects of the game. Where are the best teas on the circuit?

PN: Derby used to have good food, but Lord's for twenty-plus years has been the leader.

TMS : What does the future hold for you now you have retired? Carlisle United matches? After-dinner speaking?

PN: I'm an ambassador for LCCC and PCA, and my autobiography, *Keeping Quiet*, came out in July 2012 via The History Press, so I have been busy with that. I'm a director of Super Skills Travel Cricket Division. I'm also involved with Port St George www.portstgeorge. com and the after-dinner circuit up and down the country which is fun. Maybe a Carlisle United takeover in the future! Blue army!

Paul, you've been a legend and thank you for your time. If anyone reading this would like to hire Paul out for his hilarious after-dinner speaking, then get in touch and we will happily point you his way. It will certainly liven up any club dinner.

IS SLEDGING A NEW PHENOMENON IN CRICKET OR HAS IT BEEN GOING ON FOR YEARS?

Fred Trueman, a man who never liked runs coming off his bowling, was playing for England in the 1950s and Raman Subba Row let one go through his legs, which went for four. At the end of the over, Row sidled up to Fiery Fred and apologised saying, 'Sorry, I should have kept my legs together', to which the Yorkshireman replied, 'Aye, so should your mother!'

There was also the case of Douglas Jardine who entered the Australian dressing room during the infamous Bodyline series to complain to Bill Woodfull, the Aussie skipper, that he had been called a bastard. Woodfull demanded hush, before asking the question of his team, 'Which of you bastards called this bastard a bastard?'

So the point is, it has been happening since at least the 1930s, and no doubt longer. Incidents involving W.G. Grace are legendary and for as long as batsmen have been hitting bowlers, no doubt sledging has occurred. In my view, sledging at club level is getting worse, less humorous and the standard 'Fuck off, you're shit, etc, etc' is becoming increasingly common. Part of the problem is that in cricket the likelihood of physical retribution is rare, unlike in football and rugby.

Some of the more amusing sledges are quite acceptable and the masters of this trade seem to be those who have worn the baggy green cap of Australia. Merv Hughes springs to mind in the West Indies, and as usual in their dominant era, the Master Blaster Viv Richards was taking him apart. Viv hit him for four 4s in one over, and a riled Merv stopped halfway down the track before farting loudly. 'Let's see you hit that one to the boundary!' roared the moustachioed paceman to a dumbfounded Richards.

Mark Waugh, known as Afghanistan (the forgotten Waugh), wasn't selected for Australia for years, while brother Steve was making his mark with bat and ball for the Wallabies. Mark was another who liked to dish out the verbals, but was known to not be able to take them very well. On England's tour of Australia a few years back, he started on number eleven James Ormond, telling him in no uncertain terms that he wasn't good enough to play for England, to which Ormond replied 'Maybe not, but at least I'm the best player in my family.'

Dennis Lillee and Rod Marsh were a couple of others who liked a chat, especially Lillee, although Javed Miandad wasn't overly impressed with the cut of his jib in a Test in 1982.

I, myself, have been the victim of sledging, and have dished it out over the years, and Liam was one of my co-conspirators. In a game where we needed to win to get promoted a few years ago, we had posted a total of about 180, and the other side were 90–6. Before we knew it, the skipper and his sixteen-year-old son, aided and abetted by some overly aggressive field placements from the skipper (me), had rattled their score to nearer the 150 mark. Something urgent needed to be done, and nothing works as well as a good sledge! I wasn't in a position to deliver the sledge personally as I was the skipper, I had known their skipper for years, and anyway it's not the done thing for a man in his thirties to sledge a young lad. Instead I instructed my youngest player (Liam, my co-author) to unsettle the younger lad by any means possible. This he did and within two balls the young lad had tried to smash one out of the ground, only to be caught at mid-off. As we were all celebrating the wicket, the skipper came up to me and said to me, 'Your bowler has just called my son a c**t'. I then called the Liam over, asked him if he had said this to which he nodded his head sheepishly, and made him apologise to the skipper. Not only did I instigate the whole thing, but then I made him apologise for it as well. Needless to say, we got the remaining wickets extremely cheaply and won comfortably, going on to win promotion. I am not proud of it, but sometimes you just have to resort to extreme measures!

STEVE KIRBY, THE KING OF BANTER

Steve Kirby is a man who comes with a reputation. So when I spoke with him recently, the morning after a Somerset defeat, I was slightly worried he'd be pissed off, in a bad mood and we'd not get the greatest interview. I shouldn't have worried: the man is a legend. He loves his cricket, and loves his banter and the only thing I have to worry about judging by the amount he talked, is the size of my phone bill from a certain company which shares its name with the colour of Kirbs' hair.

TMS: Kirbs, it must be a privilege to be asked by such a classy publication as The Middle Stump to do a Q & A?

SK: Absolutely. I am totally honoured. I'm joining an exclusive band of cricketers and hope I can do it justice.

TMS: What do you think of the site so far?

SK: It has come highly recommended by Foxy Fowler. The banter is fantastic and I just hope I don't let the side down!

TMS: What's going on down at Somerset with all the injuries? Too much cider?

SK: Not enough, mate. Not enough Thatchers! We need to get more down our Gregory Pecks! The apples strengthen the bones, so if the likes of Tres had drunk more, he wouldn't have done his ankle in. No, we need to drink more of it.

TMS: You've just come back from injury yourself, haven't you?

SK: I played two or three one-dayers last week in the 2nd XI. I was told I'd be out for six weeks, and I'm ahead of schedule as that was five and-a-half weeks ago. I played in a CB40 yesterday. Healing comes from plenty of cider!

TMS: What was the Champions Trophy like to play in 2011?

SK: Unbelievable. You couldn't catch your breath. They are fanatical in India. I had been there before with the England Lions but their support of the IPL sides is unreal. We checked into our hotel for five days thinking we'd be on our way home and we stayed for three-and-a-half weeks! We beat the Kolkata Knight Riders and we needed our guard to get out of the hotel, I tell you. Not that we'd have got hurt, but they are just fanatical. Hyderabad was mental – you couldn't hear yourself think. There were blokes screaming like women, and 50,000 of them. You can imagine the noise.

TMS: When we spoke to Somerset Chairman Andy Nash he said the team spirit was great among you guys. We're going to ruin that now by asking you to name who is the worst dressed at Somerset?

SK: A lot of people say me, but I am a stylish and classy individual. I will have to go for Gemaal Hussain, God bless him! He's got this car, a Honda Prelude which is bright yellow and it looks shocking. He went all the way to Scotland to get it. Why go all that way to pick up that piece of shit? Compo (Nick Compton) is not the best either. He wears these white trousers. He also has issues on the wardrobe front!

TMS: Who can drink the most and the least on the circuit in your opinion?

SK: Could well be me. We're not huge drinkers these days. I hated it when I was young and people would say 'in my day it was different', but really it is completely different now. We have a drinks list where people will order a Coke during a game, but if you ordered a Guinness or a Thatchers, they would look at you like you were a pisshead. Now you have to pick your time to have a few. It is a shame as often we are straight back on the coach after, and you don't get a chance to have a couple after the game, and people just think 'Who is that ginger idiot?' instead of getting to know me after a couple in the bar. You can also learn a lot from the opposition over a couple of beers as well.

TMS: Which of your teammates has pulled the worst-looking bird?

SK: I really can't answer that! There have been some stinkers but I really cannot say in public!

TMS: You've been known to bowl the odd short one and follow it up with a few words. Who else has got good banter?

SK: Not me. My banter is rubbish. Jos Buttler, for a young pup, has good banter, and I am going to hate myself for saying this but Pete Trego is superb. On his day he is one of the funniest blokes in cricket. Anthony McGrath at Yorkshire is good too, very sharp.

TMS: Any truth in the rumour that in his last match you said to Athers that you'd seen 'better batters in a fish and chip shop'? And if so, that is fucking quality!

SK: That is true, yes. At the time with him, it went down really badly – like a shit sandwich. However, I got him out twice in that match so it must have worked. He just wanted to get away from me. He must have thought, 'who is this ginger lunatic?'

TMS: What is the best sledge given/received?

SK: I take some unbelievable shit as I dish it out. We were playing Lancashire once at Headingley when I was at Yorkshire, and Chris Schofield was batting. He had about 40-odd not out, and everything was behind square – he hadn't hit it in front of square. He kept squirting me down to third man, so I said to the umpire, 'Right, I'm coming round the wicket, and call an ambulance.' He said, 'Pardon?' I said, 'Right arm around the wicket, and call a fucking ambulance.' Ryan Sidebottom and Silvers (Chris Silverwood) were pissing themselves laughing. Anyway, you can guess what I bowled next? I've slipped him a bouncer, but it was so slow Schofield had time for his tea and biscuits before pulling me for six into the West Stand. Some old boy from Barnsley was there eating his sandwiches with a flask of tea, and it has hit him straight on the head, knocked him clean out, so we had to call an ambulance after all!

TMS: Who is the quickest you have faced? And seen?

SK: Every bowler to me is quick. I get pinned every other time I bat. My helmet is my most important piece of equipment. However, I was playing for Yorkshire on a quick deck at Chester-le-Street, and Shoaib Akhtar frightened the shit out of me. He'd gone through our top order and Goughie was out and not very helpfully told me he couldn't see him! He really was bowling at the speed of light. I was batting with Craig White who had about 80-odd and he didn't want to face him. Anyway, he hit me a few times in the ribs, and Nicky Peng was at short leg shouting out, 'You're not going to believe what he's calling you.' I was saying. 'Shut the fuck up!' and Peng told him I had called him the Rawalpindi Tuk Tuk, as opposed to the Rawalpindi Express, which I had. Next ball he has beamed me, and quick, which nearly killed me, so I've gone and had words, and tried to punch him. Harmy pulled me back, Craig White pulled me back – it was chaos. Next ball was a bouncer that the Colonel, Phil Mustard, behind the sticks didn't even get a paw on, and it hit the sightscreen and bounced all the way back to him! He didn't get me out though!

TMS: You were selling industrial flooring weren't you and must have thought your chance had passed you by when Leicestershire released you? Have you got any advice to youngsters who are on the fringes of the professional game?

SK: Never ever give in. If you have a dream – hang on, this sounds like Martin Luther King, doesn't it? Seriously, if you have a dream, then go for it. Not many people get a second chance in sport. I'm thirty-four now, and one of my dreams is to play for England. I might not make it, but I will never, ever give up.

TMS: Being a ginger lad, how do you cope with being exposed to the sun on a regular basis?

SK: Always, always put a sun block on, no matter what the weather.

TMS: Have you been taught anything about it?

SK: I've been very lucky. I had a melanoma removed. The PCA came round and scanned us under the ultraviolet light. I looked about eighty-five!

TMS: What do you think of Factor 50 and the work they do?

SK: If there was a Factor 120 I'd use it! Seriously, any charity that can make people aware are fantastic and doing a great job.

TMS: Tea is an extremely important part of the game. Where are the best teas in your opinion?

SK: Lord's. Without a shadow. You get a menu of three or four choices. The whole experience of playing there is great. Somerset are there this week, and I'm gutted to miss it. Not for the cricket, but for the food!

TMS: Best three youngsters coming through in the country?

SK: Jos Buttler. A fantastic striker of a cricket ball. Very talented. Ben Stokes is an exceptional talent up at Durham, and I like Tymal Mills at Essex, but the guy I really like is Stuart Meaker at Surrey. He's bowling very well and Lewey (Jon Lewis) is my mate, and reckons he has all the attributes needed to succeed. He hit me on the pads last year, and I've fucking hobbled off. He's quick.

TMS: What will you do after you have finished in the game?

SK: Stay in coaching. Try to complete my Level Four badge. Although, maybe I'll go into marketing? Anywhere I can talk shit with people and have a beer. I'm good at that!

TMS: Steve, it's been an absolute pleasure.

SK: Thank you, and sorry for talking the hind legs off a donkey.

: Look after yourself Dan, and look forward to catching up over a
: Thatchers when you come down here.

: **TMS**: Definitely.

And with that, Kirbs was gone, and no doubt ready to unleash his special brand of banter onto someone else. Characters like him are what cricket is about, and it was a pleasure and a privilege to talk to him.

GETTING PINNED

Here The Middle Stump goes through incidents which have shown the world that cricket can be a dangerous pastime at times. Facing any quick can get the juices flowing, but we recount some of the incidents that have actually hospitalised people.

1. **ANDY LLOYD**, 1984

   The West Indies were at their most supreme in 1984 and in Malcolm Marshall possessed one of the finest bowlers of all time. Andy Lloyd was an up-and-coming left-hander from Warwickshire and after half an hour of ducking and weaving the quicks, ducked into a bouncer from Marshall. Helmets back then weren't what they are now and young Mr Lloyd ended up in hospital for three days. However, it has given him a claim to fame as the only opening batsman never to be out in Test cricket, but he sadly ended up with just the one cap. Amazingly, Wikipedia claims he is no relation of Clive Lloyd! Well, they were both left-handed I suppose ...

2. **TWO BROTHERS**, 1985

   A cricketing story of folklore is told in North London about two brothers who played for Winchmore Hill CC. One was a quick left-armer who represented Middlesex schools and who would have been about seventeen, while his brother a decent player who was fifteen. The older one bet the younger one he wouldn't deliberately head away a bouncer without a helmet on, and the younger one foolishly took him up on this wager. Although £10 was quite a lot of money back then, no pain could make up for the younger brother being on the deck for a good half an hour, having purposely headed a cricket ball. Who knows if he ever paid up?

3. EWAN CHATFiELD, 1975

Having been given a thorough going-over by Thommo and Lillee, England had a couple of Tests bolted on to the end of a long winter by touring New Zealand. Ewan Chatfield was a genuine ferret, one who goes in after the rabbits, and thoroughly pissed off with him holding them up in a partnership with Geoff Howarth, Lancashire's Peter Lever slipped him a bouncer. It hit Chatfield on the temple, before the days of wearing a lid, and he swallowed his tongue. CPR Vinnie Jones-style by England physio Bernie Thomas saved his life, and Lever was in tears for hours after. Allegedly after he saw him in hospital, Chatfield told Lever he looked better than he did! Chatfield never bowled another bouncer in his life after that!

4 JUSTiN LANGER, 2006

Langer celebrated his 100th Test by copping one early doors of the skiddy Makhaya Ntini. Whether Justin remembers such a milestone is unlikely as he was off the pitch for the rest of the game. Interestingly he was also pinned by West Indian Ian Bishop on his debut in 1992. He proceeded to retire from his role as the short leg fielder after that. For a gobby Australian, interested in kick-boxing and the like, it has to be said that Langer went down like a sack of shit, but then again, I've never been pinned by a South African pinging it down at 90mph!

5. BERTiE OLDFiELD, 1933

Aussie keeper Oldfield had the misfortune to top edge one into his face off English quick Harold Larwood in an incident which nearly severed diplomatic relations between the two countries. Larwood was the *bête noir* of the Aussie crowd, with puppetmaster Douglas Jardine instructing him to bowl to a bodyline field, which nearly caused a riot. However, this was one of the times he wasn't actually bowling to that field, and the two became close buddies after Larwood moved to Australia.

6. JOHN EDRICH AND BRIAN CLOSE, 1976

What in the blazes were two guys of forty-one and forty-six doing opening the batting for England? Trying to see out the final hour at Old Trafford, even a fired-up Michael Holding in his pomp, got bored of hitting them as they took punishment which deserved the 'We won't grovel' spiel of South African-born skipper Tony Grieg. Both got peppered, but to their credit, neither flinched. When they returned to the dressing room they both threw down their bats and threatened retirement. And their reward? Both were dropped for the next match!

7. MIKE GATTING, 1986

The perfect perfume ball was again delivered by England's nemesis, Malcolm Marshall, this time to Mike Gatting who had his nose rearranged into several fragments. The West Indies, with a four-pronged pace battery, were awesome and Allan Lamb (at the other end) actually walked when he hadn't hit one! After Gatt had been carried off, Windies skipper Viv Richards went to polish the ball, and found shards of the Middlesex man's nose embedded in it. However, the most amusing aspect of this story is that when a black-eyed Gatt faced a press conference, the first question he received was 'So where exactly did it hit you?'

8. TERRY JENNER, 1971

Shane Warne's coach Jenner obviously didn't teach him the ins and outs of facing a genuine quick, as future poet John Snow pinned him good and proper in 1971. The ball actually rebounded quite a long way back out through the covers, off Jenner's forehead, before a finger-wagging row occurred between Aussie umpire Rowan and the no-nonsense Yorkshireman Ray Illingworth. Snow was then grabbed by the crowd trying to pull him in, to give him a good hiding, before Illy took his boys off the pitch under a hail of bottles! Nice.

9. GARY KIRSTEN AND ANDREW HUDSON, 1994

Talking of Illy, the man infamously referred to as Malcolm Devon was seriously fired up at The Oval in '94. After being pinned himself by a Fanie de Villiers bouncer, he told the South Africans, Schwarzenegger-style 'You guys are history', after the slip cordon were found chuckling at him. You could literally see the brown patches on the back of Kirsten and Hudson's whites, as the Derbyshire quick gave them a serious going-over when it was his turn to bowl. England won comfortably with Devon (or was it Malcolm?), picking up 9-57.

10. IAN BOTHAM, 1974

Beefy took a blow straight into the mouth during a one-day game, off the hardly pedestrian Anderson Roberts. He simply spat out a couple of teeth and carried on. Needless to say, they won the game and the legend was born. It was nothing compared to the pain the English press put him though in the 1980s.

ALEX TUDOR

Alex Tudor was one of the most talented all-rounders in English cricket back in the late 1990s. But for a career-ending knee problem, the man they call Bambi would have no doubt had a long-standing international career. No less a judge than Steve Waugh was impressed with him during his tour to Australia, and he still holds the highest score by an English nightwatchman with 99 not out against New Zealand. His enthusiasm for the game still shines through, and now he runs excellent coaching camps, where he is a role model to the future generation. Here he talks to The Middle Stump about that knock, quick bowlers and why Graham Thorpe should never visit Wandsworth.

TMS: Thanks for agreeing to the interview with us Alex. It must be a huge privilege?

AT: It is massive. I've seen and heard good things. I saw the good banter with Rikki Clarke, a good friend of mine, who was made captain of the Ugly XI. Rikki has a great sense of humour. No, it is an exciting new project, and an exciting new piece of cricketing literature for cricket lovers out there.

TMS: So which features higher – a 99 for England or being asked to do a Q & A with us?

AT: A trick question. Unfortunately, England winning the Test match v New Zealand.

TMS: It was the highest score by an English nightwatchman. Is that still the case?

AT: I believe so, for England yes. Jason Gillespie got a 200 v Bangladesh but it was only Bangladesh, and mine was against a proper attack.

TMS: Do you hold it against Graham Thorpe for arsing up your ton?

AT: As the years go on, it hurts more and more to be honest. As a twenty-one-year-old kid, I was just happy to win the Test match. Back in 1999 it was a tough time, we'd just been bundled out of the World Cup, Bumble had gone as coach, and Alec as skipper, so to get a win I was just over the moon. As Graham put in his book, he was in a different and difficult place back then, so no, I don't hold it against him. As long as he stays away from Wandsworth, he'll be ok. Especially from my mum!

TMS: Did he buy you a drink to say sorry?

AT: Graham Thorpe buy a drink? Another trick question. He never buys a drink. He's got short arms and long pockets – and he *does* have short arms, let me tell you!

TMS: Talk us through what it was like to get pinned by Brett Lee?

AT: Not nice. If you dish it out, you have to take it, and I did dish it out. We had a decent duel, and I had peppered him when he batted. When I came out to bat he said, 'Tudor, I owe you some' and he did give it to me. It was one of the quickest spells I have seen. Tres gloved one down the leg side and ran off, so what chance did I have when someone of the class of Marcus Trescothick does that? Glenn McGrath was chirping up from mid-off big time, and Brett banged one in with the new ball, that didn't really bounce. I ducked and it pinned me – went through the grille. I thought I had lost my eye. Brett being the good man he was, came over to see me, and also came up to me after the game. We had a good rapport.

TMS: Did the helmet take any of the impact?

AT: Yeah, luckily it clipped the top of the helmet. What a lot of people don't know is that it wasn't my lid. I was only playing as I was out there, I was at the Academy on standby, and I had an England A helmet which has a red badge. I obviously couldn't use that, so borrowed James Foster's. Fozzie's was a bit small, and not really what you want with your chin exposed facing one of the fastest blokes in the world. Thank God it hit the peak, or I'd have ended up like Colin Milburn.

TMS: How many stitches?

AT: Only three or four. There was a nice nurse, well, nice back in those days anyway, and I was lying down on the bed feeling really sorry for myself, thinking I was going to lose my eye. She said, 'Can you see?' and I said no. Then she put the TV on, and every ten minutes or so it kept coming up on the news which didn't make me feel any better.

TMS: Who else was quick?

AT: There were a few. Shoaib Akhtar, Allan Donald, Harmy, Freddie, Goughie was 90mph plus. There was more of a pack mentality to bowlers. Jason Gillespie was also quick, as was Mohammed Sami.

TMS: Who is quick now?

AT: Steve Finn for consistent pace. Dale Steyn is quick but very clever and changes pace for the conditions. When he needs to though, he bowls a heavy spell. Morkel is, like Harmy, all at your rib cage. There are some youngsters around – De Lange, Mitchell Starc, Pat Cummins – who are all quick, but they keep breaking down, which is something that needs looking at.

TMS: Who took you apart?

AT: Growing up, Paul Johnson at Notts. I said to Smokes (Adam Hollioake) that I don't want to bowl. He panned me, I had no idea what to bowl and how he never played for England I don't know. I had some good battles with Fred and everyone knows about the 38 off of one over he took me for. I did take five wickets in the first innings of that match though. Fred's hundred in a quarter-final once against us was brilliant. I had a lot of trouble with Ed Smith. He timed the nuts off of the ball and a few times, put me 'in the bush' as my dad would say!

TMS: You came through the London Schools system. Why do so few kids make it from the state sector in cricket?

AT: Are they getting the same opportunities? That's my question. Especially in London. You can't tell me with all the inner-city schools there are not that many that kick on. My brother Ray works for Capital Kids and goes into schools helping. They found Ravi Bopara. You can't tell me there is not another Ravi out there? A lot of private school kids filter into the county system, and while I'm not saying they get looked after better, there must be more state school kids out there.

TMS: What do you know about Factor 50?

AT: I knew about it through Twitter. This lady tweeted me and made me aware. Melanoma is something that is close to me and my parents as someone we knew died from it. You see Steve Bucknor and the like, and people say, 'Oh, you don't need it as you're black', but you still do. I have a kid and bathe him as soon as the sun comes out. You see the Aussies and their 'Slip, Slap, Slop' campaign and it is so important. Gill Nuttall sends out a great message and sunscreen should be in everyone's kit bag.

TMS: Were you taught anything about it as a youngster?

AT: No. A senior player might say it is hot, put some on, but no. Factor 50 and their message is vitally important.

TMS: Who had the best banter on the circuit?

AT: David Nash was top-drawer. He annoyed people, he never let up and was known for it. Nashy was good, and didn't care who you were. He was inappropriate at times, and would talk about size of anatomy and the like, but he was good.

TMS: Best teas on the circuit?

AT: Wickford CC in Essex. The best in the world. When you go there, get your overs out of the way in the morning session, or if batting, get out before lunch. They have ribs, chicken, every cake going. I've been to the MCG and Lord's, which are good, but Wickford is different gravy.

TMS: What does the future hold for Alex Tudor?

AT: Well I don't do as much weights as I used to! I'm still only thirty-four and playing a good standard of club cricket. I love playing still. I'm also an ambassador for the PCA and playing with some legends I looked up to when I was a youngster. Devon Malcolm, Nico (Paul Nixon), Phil DeFreitas, Emburey, Shaun Udal, Paul Prichard, who were all guys who played county cricket for years, and some of the stories in the changing rooms are hilarious. I run coaching camps, and I try to pass on some of the experience I gained when I played. We teach life skills as well, and getting the kids to be respectful is important. We get them to enjoy it, and if they enjoy the game as much as I did, I've done a good job.

TMS: Alex, we really appreciate you giving up your time for us and we wish you well.

AT: A pleasure and thank you.

2005's STARS OF TOMORROW

The summer of 2005 was significant for English cricket. Everyone remembers the Ashes and England winning back the little urn, but there was another series being played involving an England side. Sri Lanka under-19s arrived in Blighty for three one-day internationals and a three-Test series.

While Flintoff was knocking over Australians left, right and centre and KP was the new boy on the scene (complete with one of the worst haircuts seen in international cricket), there were some young hopefuls battling it out, each one trying to become a future England star.

We take a look at the young men involved in the Test series (which England won convincingly 3–0), and who indeed became Internationals and county pros, and who failed to live up to the potential shown as eighteen and nineteen year olds.

NB: The figures below were right up until June 2012.

1. **VARUN CHOPRA** (captain) (Essex) – Started his career at Essex, now at Warwickshire. Captained the side in 2005 and averaged 48 and since then has gone on to play numerous matches. Chopra opens the batting and has eleven centuries to his name with an average of 34.26. Made his debut in 2006.

2. **JOE DENLY** (Kent) – A product of the Kent youth system, now playing for Middlesex. Denly has been capped nine times in ODIs by England. He has a first-class average of 34.74 in 89 matches and has amassed thirteen centuries. Made his Kent debut in 2004.

3. **STEVEN DAVIS** (Worcs) – Now playing for Surrey, this opening batsman and wicketkeeper played nine ODIs for England, although played second fiddle to Matt Prior on the Test stage. Made his first-class debut in 2005 and has since played 113 matches and averages a superb 39.31. Also has 361 dismissals to his name.

4. **NICK JAMES** (Warks) – An all-rounder who didn't make his first-class debut until 2009 for Warwickshire. Now plays for Glamorgan,

where he has a chance opening the batting and bowling his left-arm spin. Averages 26 with the bat and 20 with the ball.

5. **CHRiS THOMPSON** (Surrey) – An opening batsman of some promise, some fine displays for Surrey 2nd XI gave him his chance for the under-19s. Played his only first-class game for Leicestershire against Glamorgan in 2009. Thompson played for Surrey 2nd XI again in the summer of 2012.

6. **KEViN LATOUF** (Hampshire) – Only one first-class game for this South African batsman. Played in the C&G final for Hampshire in 2005 but only played in ten more list A games.

7. **MOEEN ALi** (Warks) – Made his first-class debut in 2005 for Warwickshire. Now playing for Worcestershire he has 75 first-class matches under his belt with seven hundreds and 51 wickets. He averages 34.94 with the bat and is still only twenty-four years of age.

8. **JOHN SiMPSON** (Lancs) – Wicketkeeper Simpson made his first-class debut for Middlesex in 2009. He has played 43 first-class matches and has 131 dismissals. A left-handed bat who comes in lower down the order than most glovemen, Simpson has two first-class hundreds and an average of 31.74.

9. **STUART BROAD** (Leics) – Needs no introduction. England's opening bowler and a more than handy left-hand bat. 147 Test match wickets and a top score of 169 against Pakistan. Plays for Nottinghamshire when allowed (by England, not his mum).

10. **TOM SMiTH** (Lancs) – Made his Lancashire debut in 2005. Still with the red rose county, Smith has played 71 first-class matches with 146 wickets and a bowling average of 31.55. Handy with the bat, he has three hundreds with an average of 26.08.

11. **ADAM HARRiSON** – (Glamorgan) A promising seam bowler, Harrison only made three first-class appearances for the Welsh county. Brother of David, they became the youngest siblings to play for Glam since 1983.

12. **MARK FOOTiTT** (Notts) – Made his Nottinghamshire debut against Glamorgan in 2005, but has since moved to Derbyshire where he has played 26 matches and taken 70 wickets. Footitt is a left-arm seamer who can bowl at some licks.

13. **BEN HARMiSON** (Durham) – Brother of ex-England quick Steve, Ben now plays for Kent. Has a batting average of 26.38 and has three centuries in his 43 first-class matches.

So they were the stars of the future. Seven years on and ten are still playing county cricket, three with international experience. I wonder how many of this year's crop will still be playing county cricket in 2019? With the exciting Daniel Bell-Drummond and captain Adam Ball, you would hope that many, if not all will have a successful career in cricket. Who knows, we might even have the next Stuart Broad in the ranks!

JASON GILLESPIE

It's not often you get to catch up with a member of what was probably the best side to ever walk onto a cricket pitch. So when we spoke recently with the opening bowler of that side, it was a huge privilege. I had been told by a couple of our previous interviewees that he was a good guy, and having now spoken with Jason Gillespie, I have to agree. We caught up with him in 2012, the season he led Yorkshire to promotion at the first attempt. Now coaching at Yorkshire CCC, the straight-talking

Australian spoke to The Middle Stump about coaching, wine and that famous 201 – the highest score by a nightwatchman.

TMS: Jason, thanks for agreeing to have a chat with us. Having played for one of the best sides the cricketing world has ever seen, it must be a huge honour to appear in The Middle Stump?

JG: Haha, yes, an absolute privilege.

TMS: What do you think of the blog so far?

JG: It's been interesting. Anything that promotes cricket is good in my book.

TMS: How are things up in Yorkshire?

JG: We've had some challenging times already this year, but we're moving in the right direction. We have a strong team and if we play to our ability we can challenge anyone.

TMS: You have some great youngsters up there with the likes of Joe Root, Jonny Bairstow, Adil Rashid?

JG: Yeah we do. It's exciting to see these guys perform for Yorkshire. They prepare well, they work hard for themselves and for me, and they have a great desire from within which is pleasing from a coaching perspective.

TMS: Is there a pressure to bring success to a club like Yorkshire with their history, and with them having won thirty-one County Championship titles?

JG: I don't feel pressure. I believe 100 per cent our players will do the job, they prepare really well and what will be will be. Destiny is in our own hands. If you let pressure get to you, then you never perform to the best of your ability.

TMS: Do you miss playing?

JG: No. Not one minute of any day do I miss it!

TMS: Not even as part of the great Australian side you played in?

JG: Well I loved it. I had a great time professionally and personally but no, I don't miss playing.

TMS: Who would win if that Aussie side took on the West Indians of the 1980s?

JG: You just can't compare, we are from different eras. The West Indies were a great side, so let's just leave it as it is.

TMS: So talk to us about your 201?

JG: I just got lucky.

TMS: It was your birthday wasn't it? I bet you got pissed that night?

JG: Ha. Yeah it was my birthday. Maybe after the game we had a couple of quiet ones, as you do! I knew it was my last game to be honest, I knew my time was up.

TMS: And you have a wine called 201 – is that right?

JG: Dizzy 201 wines – they're selling well all around the world.

TMS: And are they from Barossa Valley?

JG: They're South Australian wines, yes.

TMS: Who is the quickest you have seen/faced?

JG: I really couldn't split Brett Lee or Shaun Tait.

TMS: A couple of the Glamorgan boys were saying facing Tait was frightening.

JG: Yeah, he is seriously quick, mate.

TMS: Best sledge you have heard?

JG: James Ormond. He came out to bat and Mark Waugh started on him from slip, asking him why he should be here, etc. Quick as a flash, he came back with 'At least I'm the best player in my family', to which we all rolled up laughing at.

TMS: Who could drink the most or the least on the circuit?

JG: We're all professional athletes! I dunno, who counts when you're having a couple of drinks with friends.

TMS: Best food on the circuit?

JG: All I will say is this year I haven't had a good one!

TMS: Are Aussie kids taught more about sun protection than English kids do you think?

JG: Yes they are. It is more ingrained in the culture, and the fact that the weather is so different over there, it means that they are.

TMS: And obviously you know about Factor 50? What do you think of the work they do?

JG: They send out a very important message. The work they do is crucial, and I wholeheartedly applaud what they are doing.

TMS: Why are England successful now as opposed to in previous eras?

JG: A number of reasons. They are giving guys a run, they're picking players and sticking with them. They have an excellent attack and they can bowl sides out. The batting unit is settled and they're scoring runs. If you bowl sides out and score runs, you'll win games. It's a simple game really!

TMS: Who are the best youngsters coming through in England?

JG: I don't really want to name names, but there are lots of good players coming through at the moment.

TMS: What do the next few months hold for you?

JG: Travelling around with Yorkshire and trying to win a few games!

TMS: Jason, thank you very much for your time and hopefully we'll have a glass of wine, maybe Dizzy 201, when we catch up?

JG: An absolute pleasure. Best of luck.

'HAVE YOU HEARD OF MATTHEW MAYNARD . . . ?'

'Have you heard of Matthew Maynard/He's my favourite cricketer/ I would rather watch him play than pick up my guitar'. Lyrics from 'Mr Carbohydrate' by the Manic Street Preachers.

Not many players have had their name in song lyrics, but Matthew Maynard is a man with a difference, and during our chat with him, came across as a top bloke. Here The Middle Stump, spoke with the ex-Glamorgan man about cricket, coaching, beers and what Ricky Ponting actually said to Duncan Fletcher back in May 2012.

TMS: Thanks for agreeing to do a Q & A with The Middle Stump. You must be honoured?

MM: A huge privilege. Seriously, it is modern journalism, and for a read, it is right up there.

TMS: So what do you think of the blog so far?

MM: What I like about it is that it is light-hearted but has some serious stuff in there as well. Great stuff.

TMS: Do you miss playing?

MM: Not at all. Towards the end I was working in insurance for a place in Caerphilly, and then I got the job with Duncan Fletcher. I knew my time had come to an end. I loved playing, but knew my time was up.

TMS: The days with Duncan must have been great with the 2005 Ashes-winning side. What did Ponting actually say when Gary Pratt ran him out?

MM: 'You fucking cheat, Fletcher' were his words as he was legging it up the steps. The thing is the Aussies did it all the time, and Pratt wasn't playing much at Durham, and was a brilliant fielder, so we picked him. He became the star of the tour bus that year!

TMS: Obviously the coaching career is going well in South Africa with Nashua Titans winning their four-day and T20 competitions?

MM: We have a good group of players but it is managing them in and out of their international commitments. Sometimes they are physically tired, sometimes they are mentally jaded. It is tough on them to go from internationals to first-class cricket, and often it isn't physical, but they need mental rejuvenation.

TMS: What the bloody hell is going on down at Glamorgan this year?

MM: They have struggled, haven't they? It is very tough on Mark Wallace, who is a good guy. We did warn them that bringing in the likes of Alviro Petersen would create problems, but they need stability, and obviously they're missing James Harris. It looks like, by their signings, that they were going for the T20 trophy this year.

TMS: Who was the maddest you played with or against?

MM: I played with him and against him: Phil Tufnell. I roomed with him in the Caribbean and the guy does not stop. Loves a drink and a ciggie! A very funny guy.

TMS: Best sledge received?

MM: Shane Warne at The Oval in '93. As I came out to bat, I was needing a score to get on the tour of the West Indies and a plane was flying overhead. Warnie said, 'You'd best get some runs mate, or you won't be getting on one of those this winter,' pointing at the plane. It completely threw me.

TMS: Steve James says you like a beer, and Phil Tufnell said you ruined him on the Brains Skull Attack down in Cardiff a few times. Who could drink the most and the least on the circuit?

MM: Geoff Holmes was a two-pot screamer. Two lager shandies and he was finished, but he was a great roommate. He would wake me up after a night out, as he was in bed by 9.00 p.m. We never saw each other though! As for the best, I think I inherited a gene from my father where I never get hangovers. I grew up in the Liverpool Arms in Menai Bridge in Anglesey, so maybe I learned early? Jason Gillespie can put it away.

TMS: Who was the quickest you ever faced?

MM: Depended on how 'tired' I was from the night before. Ian Bishop bowled me a quick spell at Chesterfield one year, and Allan Donald bowled some quick spells at me. I used to hate the dobbers, though. People like Ronnie Irani, who you'd smash for a quick twenty or so, then they'd get you out.

TMS: Best teas on the circuit?

MM: Everyone says Lord's but Derby used to be so shit we'd always go for a takeaway. Then one year they got a new chef in, and his lamb was superb. You saw how much weight John Morris put on? That's how good they were. I think he put on about 5 stone in one season!

TMS: What were you taught about sun protection when you played?

MM: I played in New Zealand and got caught badly when I was about twenty, on a cloudy day, and got really burnt. It was a real eye-opener, and I don't tend to burn. After that, I always wore long sleeves and a floppy hat. The guys now, especially in South Africa, are good and slap it on before every session.

TMS: What do you think of Factor 50 and the work they do promoting skin cancer awareness via cricket?

MM: Fantastic. Any awareness is invaluable. It is important they go into schools as those issues are critical. Every school should stock at least Factor 30+ and a hat. Cricketers are much better educated these days, thanks to the likes of them.

TMS: Not many players have had their name in song lyrics?

MM: Haha! I know Nicky Wire. To have them write the song was an honour, although in the verse before they talk about being a 'boring fuckhead'.

TMS: Talking of singing, Foxy Fowler has asked us to ask you about the singing at the Level 4 coaching course …

MM: There were a great bunch on there, a few musicians with Fox on the drums. I got up and sang 'Teddy Bear' by Elvis, although I talked most of the way through it. I don't think I'll end up back in the Bangor Cathedral choir! My voice hasn't been the same since Devon Malcolm hit me in the throat in nets in the Caribbean. Keith Fletcher wanted to give him a fitness test and no one wanted to face him on a dodgy surface, so I put my hand up. Unfortunately

I couldn't get my hands up quickly enough to one from just short of a length! He's a great bloke, Devon, and I see him often through the work at the PCA.

TMS: Steve James wrote recently about selfishness in cricket. Do you think England's recent success has been down to lack of selfishness?

MM: Yes. Putting the team first is the key. Some guys don't benefit the team. I played with guys who sulked when we won because they had got a low score, or were happy when we lost as they had scored runs. I can't stand that, and I don't like those people in my teams. Steve James was always a good team man.

TMS: Best youngsters coming through in England?

MM: Everyone is talking about Jonny Bairstow, although I haven't seen that much of him. Stuart Meaker is like a young Goughie. He's quick and Chris Adams looks after him and Jade well down there.

TMS: Matt, it has been an absolute pleasure and I wish you every success. We'll buy you a Brains or three when we come down to Cardiff.

MM: That'd be great, and thank you.

GOWER'S GLORIOUS SUMMER

Let me take you back to 1985, when Gorby came to power in the old USSR, the French showed how they were a force to be reckoned with by sinking a Greenpeace boat in Auckland, football had disasters at Bradford and at Heysel, while we rocked to Live Aid at Wembley and Philadelphia.

In the charts that summer we had number ones by Sister Sledge with 'Frankie' and Eurythmics with 'There must be an Angel', while Madonna kept us pubescent teenage boys entertained with 'Into the Groove'. However, the man who was really into the groove that long, hot summer was David Ivon Gower, as he caressed the Australian bowling to all parts, stroking the ball to the boundary, while we were stroking other things over the 'Into the Groove' video!

HEADINGLEY

Aus 331 and 324
Eng 533 and 123–5

We started at Headingley in June: no May Tests then, no IPL to fit in, no T20 clogging up the screens, just three one-day internationals as an hors d'oeuvre, before the main course of Test matches were served. Gower had already made a hundred in the final one of these at Lord's as England lost 2–1. Anyway, I digress – back to Leeds where England won the first Test by five wickets.

Andrew Hilditch, a man who has had more trouble hooking than when Abu Hamza wipes his arse, was the mainstay of the Baggy Green innings with a patient 119. Norman 'Flash' Cowans opened for England, with Graham Gooch surprisingly chipping in with two wickets. A brilliant 175 from Tim Robinson was the mainstay of the England innings with fifties from Botham, resplendent with dyed blonde mullet, and Paul Downton. Hilditch again got an 80 in the second dig, with 91 from keeper Wayne Phillips, as John Emburey took 5–82. This left England needing 123 for victory and despite a few wobbles, they achieved it five wickets down.

LORD'S
Eng 290 and 261
Aus 425 and 127–6

In a mirror image of Headingley, the Aussies won by four wickets at the home of cricket. Gower showed us glimpses of what was to come as he hit a serene 86, while a young Craig McDermott took 6–70 for the Aussies. Captain Allan Border was the hero for them, with a patient 196 off 448 balls which seemed to take forever, while Botham toiled for 5–109, mullet bouncing as he ran in to the crease.

In England's second knock, Botham smashed 85, and despite Mike Gatting holding the innings together with 75 not out, they couldn't cope with the leg spin of veteran Bob Holland. The Aussies stumbled to victory, thanks to their skipper with 41 not out, as they reached 127 for the loss of six wickets.

TRENT BRIDGE
Eng 456 and 196–2
Aus 539

In the days before the new stands went up, Trent Bridge believe it or not, was a batsman's paradise, and Gower played the way only Gower could, with a delightful 166 full of lazy cover drives, swivel pulls and graceful clips off the legs. A young Geoff Lawson took 5–103 for the Australians.

In reply, Graeme Wood with 172 and Greg Ritchie with 146 gave the Aussies a first innings lead, as the Middlesex spin twins of Emburey and Edmonds bowled a mere 121 overs between them in the innings. The match petered out into a tame draw with Tim Robinson, on his home ground, boosting his average with 77 not out.

OLD TRAFFORD

Aus 257 and 340–5
Eng 482–9 dec

A rain-affected Test at Manchester this time, as England started well with Botham taking 4–79 as they skittled the Aussies out for 257. The only resistance came from David Boon with 61. England responded with 482–9, Mike Gatting continuing his fine form with a 160.

Again, the dogged, stubborn Border resisted England as he ground out 146 not out, this time with Phil Edmonds bowling a mere 54 overs, and John Emburey 51.

EDGBASTON

Aus 335 and 142
Eng 595–5

Australia batted first and thanks to South African import Kepler Wessels (see, they were doing it as well as England!) with 83, and with help down the order from opening bowlers Geoff Lawson and Craig McDermott, they amassed a respectable 335. However, they hadn't banked on the fine form of the English batting as Tim Robinson and skipper Gower put on 330 for the second wicket.

Gower's 215 was his highest Test score, to add to the double hundred he scored against India six years earlier, also at Edgbaston, and it remains one of the finest innings I have witnessed. Robinson got 148, while Gatt chipped in with a ton too. The demoralised Aussies then showed only weak resistance as the king of swing, Richard Ellison, helped himself to four wickets to add to his first innings 6, as the Aussies were rattled out for just 142. They looked as if they were holding England up, but the bizarre dismissal of Wayne Phillips killed them off. The keeper cut Emburey into silly point Allan Lamb's boot, while our imported South African took evasive action. The ball ricocheted off of his spikes into the welcoming hands of skipper Gower, without the ball touching the floor, much to the ire of Phillips, who, judging by my lip-reading skills said 'Steady up old boy, I don't really think I was out', or something along those lines, and England were on their way to going 2–1 up in the series.

THE OVAL
Eng 464
Aus 241 and 129 f/o

The Oval, long before it was the Fosters Oval, or the Kia Oval, just The Oval, was the scene of England celebrations. It was just a 351 stand for the second wicket this time, but between Gooch and Gower. The antithesis of stroke play, Gooch clubbing his cudgel, while Gower wafted his wand, saw them eventually finish on 196 and 157 respectively. The rest of the English innings fell away somewhat as they were dismissed for 464.

When it came to the Aussie turn to bat, they couldn't cope with Richard Ellison again, his ginger moustache bristling with the sniff of wickets, and his five wickets made the Antipodeans follow on. A pathetic 129 was all they achieved in their second knock, and when Les Taylor (whose moustache was also bristling, along with Botham's, Gooch's and Lamb's) had Murray Bennett caught and bowled, the Ashes were England's.

England also won the battle of the 'taches with Gooch, Lamb, Gatt, Botham, Ellison and Taylor outgunning Wood, Border, Boon, Holland and Phillips!

GARETH REES AND THE YEAR OF THE DRAGON

2012 was the Chinese Year of the Dragon, and with Wales winning rugby's Grand Slam, another Welshman was about to try to continue the Principality's sporting *annus mirabilis*. Gareth Rees is one of the most talked-about young batsmen on the county circuit. The Glamorgan left-hander is certainly being bigged-up in the press as a future England player and was picked for the MCC v the County Champions, Lancashire, at the start of the season in a match often looked upon as a trial.

The Middle Stump caught up with him while he was in Abu Dhabi at the start of the 2012 season, and tweeting Robert Croft abuse about the standard of his hotel room in Canterbury. Here, the twenty-six-year-old opening bat tells us about birds, booze and Jason Gillespie's wine-drinking, mixed in with a few serious cricketing questions.

TMS: You must be very honoured to be selected for The Middle Stump Q & A? What did you think of the Paul Nixon interview?

GR: Massive honour to be asked by The Middle Stump to do a Q & A! I'm assuming after having Nico do one, you thought you'd have to go someone a little younger for next time and with a bit more hair so went with me, ha! Nico is a top bloke and as was the case when I played against him, I had a little chuckle at a lot of what he had to say; he was great player to play against and learn from.

TMS: Congratulations on Wales' Grand Slam by the way. I understand that you played for Wales at rugby at junior level? What made you choose a career in cricket as opposed to rugby?

GR: Yeah, played a bit of rugby for Wales under-17 and Scarlets under-21s and things. I love rugby. I didn't necessarily choose a cricket career, I didn't really have the rugby as a career option. Sadly I missed the Grand Slam game as I was stuck in a Spanish airport for 12 hours waiting for a delayed flight home with Glamorgan! Gutted!

TMS: Where does your nickname of Gums come from? Is it down to your technique with the ladies?

GR: Not quite sure how gums would help with any sort of technique with the ladies! Think it came from me being quite mouthy when I started with Glamorgan and maybe a few dodgy player profile pics!

TMS: Who on the county circuit can drink the most beers? And who can put away the least?

GR: Think I'd have to say Jason Gillespie enjoyed a glass of vino like no man I've ever come across and even has his own brand, the Dizzy 201, made in honour of his highest Test score! I think another Aussie has to take the title of worst drinker – our coach Matthew Mott – a couple of shandies and he's nowhere!

TMS: Who is the best-dressed player you have shared a dressing room with?

GR: Best dressed has to go to my old teammate, Alex Wharf, a very snappy dresser!

TMS: And the worst?

GR: Worst dressed is shared by our captain, Mark Wallace, and young fast bowler James Harris. James enjoys a waistcoat and cravat option thinking he's cool, but that is one thing he sadly is not! Stick to the top of off stump, James!

TMS: Your debut was against Gloucester, I believe, at Cheltenham College a few years back? You got one, then spent what must seem like ages in the dressing room as your teammates rattled up about 800! Powell got 299, didn't he? Then Gloucester batted, followed on, so you must have spent a lifetime in the field, and you finally came in for a little cheeky 4 not out as you won by ten wickets. What was that like?

GR: I was just happy to be making my debut and it was a great experience. There was a mammoth effort from Powelly in that game and was a great Glam win. I was just happy to be a part of it, in a *very small* way!

TMS: What are the chances of an England call-up over the next year or so?

GR: Hopefully there's the chance of higher honours, which is definitely a big goal for me; I just need to make some big scores for Glam that make people really sit up and take notice. Also, if we can get success as a team, then I believe that will lead to recognition for some of our boys at a higher level.

TMS: Tea is an extremely important part of the game. Where are the best teas on the circuit?

GR: Have to agree with Nico here, Lord's is unbelievable! You just pray you're not actually batting when lunch comes around! You hope to be still in the field so that you can really take advantage of the rack of lamb, followed by the Louisiana Lovebite! World class!

TMS: Who is the quickest bowler you have faced? Have you ever literally been bricking it as someone has run into bowl?

GR: Steven Finn is probably one of the quickest I've faced in a match, but playing with Shaun Tait was unreal! I could barely see the ball being sent down by the big man! I've never really bricked facing anyone, as it's quite a buzz when you get to face someone bowling rapid, it gets the juices flowing and is quite enjoyable in a weird way!

TMS: Favourite ground to play on?

GR: Lord's is by far the best place in the world to play cricket, even lunches aside.

TMS: Ever played with a hangover?

GR: I've played the odd club game with a hangover – horrendous! Can't deal with hangovers anymore! Too old!

TMS: Name three of the best up-and-coming youngsters coming through the English (or Welsh, sorry) system?

GR: James Harris and Andrew Salter at Glamorgan and Lewis Gregory from Somerset.

TMS: Best curry house in the UK?

GR: Think I'd have to say the Cinnamon Tree in Pontcanna, Cardiff. It's a regular spot for our curry club gatherings.

TMS: Is St Helens, Swansea, still used as a county ground? Does Malcolm Nash ever turn up there, or does he still have nightmares about Sobers?

GR: Yeah, we still play at Swansea. You'd do well to hit six 6s there nowadays. I got my first hundred there, so love going back down west.

TMS: How do you think the county game will go? More T20? What are you views on the future of the County Championship?

GR: The County Championship is still the pinnacle. T20 needs its place as it's the only way the counties generate revenue, but certainly for the players the championship is what everybody wants to win in their career.

TMS: What does the next year hold for you?

GR: Hopefully it holds a couple of winners' medals with Glamorgan and an England call-up! But if not – who knows?

Gareth, you have been an absolute legend, although not sure if Messrs Harris and Wallace will think so after this! Best of luck this year and fingers crossed on that England call-up.

ENGLAND'S DEPTH: PART ONE

Go back to the '80s and early '90s and think of some of those players who were picked for England – I won't name names – as I would hate to embarrass the likes of Mark Lathwell (oops), but there was a real lack of depth to our side. We had the likes of Gooch, Gatting , Gower, Lamb and Botham coming to the end of their careers, but really we were as shallow as your average Big Brother contestant.

Nowadays English cricket has an outstanding second string and one which could probably beat most of the other sides in the world, especially in English conditions.

A quick scan of the fast bowling department reveals that we have two of the quickest bowlers in the world playing in London at present – Stuart Meaker at Surrey and Steven Finn at Middlesex. I know I am one for hyperbole, especially after a beer or three, but I write this article stone cold sober! Very different in their approach, Meaker is short and skiddy, and he certainly looked rapid through beer-goggled eyes at a game at The Oval I watched last year. Finn is more well-known, and with steepling bounce from his 6ft 7in frame, I can see batsmen's fingers in the future being broken with the same ease as a popadom at your local Indian restaurant.

Behind these two genuine pace merchants we have the Oxon oxen, Jack Brooks, who came through the route of Minor Counties cricket before landing himself a contract with Northampton and then moving to Yorkshire for 2013. Brooks tends to bowl in a headband, isn't short of a word or two and goes by the nickname of Susan Boyle! Who said characters had gone out of the game?

The fancifully named Tobias Skelton Roland-Jones at Middlesex is part of an attack that is now starting to be feared around the country, and just being around the likes of Gareth Berg, Tim Murtagh and Corey Collymore will be a great experience for him, let alone playing with and learning from Steven Finn. He currently has a more than respectable first-class career average of 22.19.

Matt Coles down at Kent was another who impressed in 2012. With a plethora of wickets and a maiden hundred, the twenty-one year old is certainly catching the eye and his future looks very bright indeed. While also in the garden of England, look out for Daniel Bell-Drummond, an eighteen-year-old who was captain at Millfield School, and last year was named Development Cricketer of the Year by the ECB.

Tymal Mills at Essex is also genuinely quick, and a decent left-arm over; something England haven't had for a number of years. Mills, a fan of The Middle Stump on Twitter, was brought into the England Lions squad last year. Essex fans are already saying he is the next John Lever!

An all-rounder to watch out for is Somerset's Lewis Gregory. The England under-19 captain can bat and bowl equally well, and broke into the Somerset team in 2012, taking advantage of an injury list the length of a Michael Holding run-up in '76! They also have the Overton twins coming through and what is absolutely brilliant about the Cidermen is that they had a dinner last season with the kids from their under-11 age group right up to those who play in the first team, all present and all wearing the same kit. One uniform, one spirit, one club!

The keeping department looks strong as well, and the likes of Jonny Bairstow have been well documented with his deserved breakthrough into the England side, but Michael Bates at Hampshire is an outstanding gloveman, and with a bit of work on his batting, will push Bairstow all the way. Having two keepers push each other, in the way that Knott and Taylor did, can only be a good thing.

With the likes of Anderson, Broad, Onions and Panesar a long way off retirement, and the return from injury of the excellent Welshman James Harris, the future looks extremely bright for English cricket.

ENGLAND'S DEPTH: PART TWO

There has been lots of talk in the press over last season of Jonny Bairstow, and he deserved his chance in the England side due to his hard-hitting approach. Another young lad from Yorkshire is also, no doubt, going to prosper for his country and that is Joe Root. The fresh-faced Root, from the same club as Michael Vaughan, Sheffield Collegiate CC, is already impressing the cricketing cognoscenti with his shots, his ability to dig in when the going gets tough (always something that appeals to the Yorkshire public), and his powers of concentration.

Talking of Michael Vaughan, James Vince down at Hampshire is reminiscent style-wise of the former England skipper, and has been similarly likened by no less a judge than Duncan Fletcher. The twenty-one year old is a product of their blooming academy at the Rose Bowl, and the stylish Vince is well thought of in Southampton. One player Hampshire have lost though, and whom Gloucestershire have gained, is Benny Howell. This lad impressed all and sundry on the difficult wickets we saw in the 2012 season. Howell, who has played in the Champions T20 Trophy, will be hoping to further his career down in Bristol.

At The Oval in 2012, Rory Hamilton-Brown and Rory Burns held together the Brown Hatters middle order, especially after the retirement of that other youngster, Mark Ramprakash! The ex-Surrey skipper, with the poshest name in cricket since Derbyshire's Ashley Harvey-Walker, was a revelation before moving back to Sussex, whilst Jason Roy, just twenty-two, is another potential King of Kennington.

At Middlesex, Joe 'Jesus' Denly has resurrected his career since moving from Canterbury, and if he keeps scoring hundreds like he did regularly in 2012, I'm sure the second coming for him as an international can't be too far away, as he proves the Doubting Thomases wrong.

Eoin Morgan needs a big season if he is to do the same. Going to the IPL has enhanced his bank balance in the short term, but playing a total of zero games out there while others made hay back in the UK for their counties, may have been a poor career move. Only time will tell.

In the West Midlands, it will be interesting to see if Varun Chopra replicates last season's good form after moving from Essex to Warwickshire a couple of years back, while Moeen Ali looks a decent player at Worcester, and he can bowl a few off-breaks. Further east, Alex Hales will make the selectors open their eyes if he scores well at Trent Bridge, and in Robin Hood's county it will be interesting to see if James Taylor can score the runs needed internationally after the rich Notts have robbed the poor of Leicestershire. While on the subject, if Josh Cobb continues his fine form for the Nottinghamshire Academy down at Grace Road, he could well come into the reckoning as well!

At Somerset, Jos Buttler and Alex Barrow are a credit to the youth system at Taunton, while Nick Compton came agonisingly close to being the first man to 1,000 runs before the end of May since Graeme Hick in 1988. Although the Compdog has been around for years, he is still only twenty-eight, and should the likes of Bell lose form or Pietersen has another meltdown, surely he deserves his chance through sheer weight of runs? Kieswetter and Hildreth are two others in that part of the world who must also be worthy of discussion.

Over in Essex and it will be interesting to see how Tom Westley and Billy Godleman fare this year. Godleman was a child prodigy, and although has had a couple of disappointing seasons, an early season hundred in 2012 could have been an indication that the twenty-three-year-old North Londoner was back to his best, but poor form meant he was eventually released and has now gone to Derby. Others worth a mention are Durham's Mark Stoneman and Glamorgan's Ben Wright.

With the people I have mentioned above, plus the seamers and keepers we wrote about in part one, English cricket has a depth we haven't seen for a number of years, if not ever. Competition for places can only be a good thing, and will push those at the top even harder to retain their places. If we want to produce a dynasty like the West Indians of twenty years ago, or the Australians of the 1990s and 2000s, and retain the number one spot for years, then strength in depth is needed, and these boys are the key to us being on top of the world for a long time to come.

England, it seems, has great riches.

The Middle Stump is going down well in dressing rooms all around the country and the Warwickshire CCC boys are some of our biggest fans. We have interviewed Rikki Clarke, and in his session he cited one man more than anyone else. That man was Steffan Piolet and we have given the twenty-year-old seamer a chance for revenge! Here he speaks to The Middle Stump's Liam and tells us about Clarke's tantrums, Richard Johnson's (lack of) banter and getting hit in the face two balls into his Championship debut.

TMS: Surely it must be an honour to be interviewed by The Middle Stump, what do you think of it so far?

SP: I like the angle of The Middle Stump. Keeping it fairly light-hearted.

TMS: I'll cut to the chase … Rikki Clarke has told us you are an awful drinker. Two-pint Piolet?

SP: Clarke deflects everything on to me in our dressing room. Yeah I'm not great, but I know my game. Laurie Evans is easily the worst.

TMS: He also told us you are the worst dancer. Surely a twenty-three-year-old with an exotic name can throw some shapes? Who is really the worst dancer?

SP: I'm not even going to deny this. I am awesome, literally awesome on my own in the shower. But because I get so much banter for being a terrible dancer, I freeze when I'm out with the lads! It's such a shame, but get me to a rave and I'm more at home.

TMS: Who is the least intelligent cricketer you have met?

SP: [Ateeq] Javid. He is *realllyy styoopid*. Rumour has it that on England under-19 duty he shouted at Ben Stokes: 'Stokes you are dumb – D - U - M- Dumb!' To be fair to him he's a very smart cricketer, but it's like all of his brain cells have gone into the game.

TMS: Who is the worst trainer at Warwickshire?

SP: Rikki Clarke when he's got 'THE HUMP'. He walks around like Ibrahimovic not getting service. Prima donna!

TMS: You have fourteen Facebook 'likes' on your Cricinfo page. I thought there would be a lot more 'Piolettes'! Who do the ladies come to watch? (Rikki has twenty-eight!)

SP: Give me a few more years … Our squad is fairly pointless on the women front. Most of them have been shacked up for years. Poor decision-making if you ask me!

TMS: Who has the best banter in county cricket and who can talk a glass eye to sleep?

SP: Chris Metters is a very funny lad actually. He's lucky in that he has a funny Devonian accent, too, so anything he says has twice the reaction. Definitely Richard Johnson has the least … top bloke, but honestly you have to meet him to see for yourself. It's impossible for any other human to have less banter – he knows it too!

TMS: On to some cricket chat. You must be happy with Warwickshire's form last season?

SP: Yeah, it's great to be in a squad which is arguably the strongest in the country. On a personal level I'm desperate to play all forms but I have to be patient as our team is clearly so strong. It's not the easiest team to get in to!

TMS: Best sledge received/dished out/heard?

SP: Sledging is, in my opinion, overrated. I've found the higher up the standard you play, the less sledging goes on. It falls on deaf ears. Sorry to disappoint!

TMS: Who is the quickest you have faced, and were you scared?

SP: I would say Tino Best on my Championship debut. He hit me in the face second ball.

TMS: Who is the most difficult person to bowl at?

SP: David Hussey, without a shadow of doubt. I like to think I can usually outwit the batsman with my variations. But that bloke seems to know EXACTLY what I'm going to bowl and when … then hits it where he wants. Class player.

TMS: The three up-and-coming youngsters in the game?

SP: Aside from the obvious ones, I'd say Richard Johnson, Ateeq Javid and Ben Brown from Sussex will be top players.

TMS: Who are the best old boys still playing?

SP: Maddy and Carter have still got it for us! Big Claude Henderson at Leicester, he's still class. God knows how old he is now!

TMS: What are your thoughts on the charity Factor 50 and the work they do?

SP: It's highly important to raise awareness. It is easy to get complacent with the sun.

TMS: Finally, what does the future hold for Steffan Piolet?

SP: A long and successful cricket career. A movie star wife, and a son who goes on to captain Tottenham. I'll take two of the three!

TMS: We would take just the one! Thanks Steffan. No doubt you will be a star.

UGLY CRICKETERS XI

We take a look at the ugliest players to have played county cricket. Beware, there are some absolute terrors in this team. So read on and see which cricketers have a face like a stuntman's knee!
In batting order, *not ranked in order of ugliness!*

1. **NASSER HUSSAiN**
   Luckily, he is now in the commentary box. A face made for radio. Someone once told Hussain, 'Don't take this the wrong way but you kind of look like Nasser Hussain.'

2. **KAMRAN AKMAL**
   Just plain ugly, no wonder we couldn't show his face on the cover of this book. Akmal is so ugly, even the tide refused to take him out.

3. **STEVE SMiTH**
   Recently voted cricket's ugliest cricketer – the only thing an Australian will win this year. He is a strong argument for eugenics.

4. **DEREK RANDALL**
   Nicknamed 'Rags', I have no doubt he pulled a few of them in his time. Randall had a nose like a builder's elbow.

5. **DAViD WARD**
   Former Surrey batsman, Ward, has a face that even Bob the Builder couldn't fix. Parents around the Home Counties still use his picture to keep children away from the fire.

6. **RiKKi CLARKE** (captain)
   Warwickshire all-rounder and one-time England faceache who is so ugly he could make onions cry. Girls have been known to tell Clarke that they wouldn't even ride him into battle.

7. LUKE RONCHi
Kept wicket for Australia now and again – most probably dropped for having a face like a blind cobbler's thumb. Plays in our side as a specialist ugly bat.

8 ALAN KNOTT (wicketkeeper)
This former England stumper has a face like a bag of smashed crabs.

9. PETER SiDDLE
Another Aussie, Siddle may be quick but his pace comes from his anger. His anger comes from having a face like a welder's bench.

10. ANDY CADDiCK
This big-eared ex-England bowler is so ugly his mum breastfed him under a blanket!

11. GRAEME WELCH
Not really a number 11, but he is that ugly. Forget about the tide, not even a sniper would take the former Derbyshire player out.

BANTER WITH RIKKI CLARKE

Rikki Clarke has good banter. We included him as captain of our Ugly XI, and he gave us plenty back on Twitter, telling me that I should be 12th man. The bloke is a top laugh, a top man and in 2012 put in some seriously top performances as Warwickshire marched to the title. If he carries on like that he will no doubt add to his England caps, and his good form was one of the main reasons why Warwickshire had such a fantastic season in 2012. Here Rikki runs through who to be wary of when they are out, who has the lowest IQ and claims he taught Graeme Swann the art of banter.

TMS: Rikki, thanks for agreeing to do a Q & A with us! Must be a huge privilege to be asked by such a classy outfit? Are you enjoying our work?

RC: When I heard that you wanted me to do this Q & A, I thought Christmas had come early. I'm definitely an A-list celebrity now. The Middle Stump is amazing and I love the humour in it.

TMS: We apologise for putting you in the Ugly XI, although may I say you are maturing well, like a fine wine. Who would you put in your ugly team?

RC: Thank you first of all for a) the selection and b) making me captain. It is an honour to be in charge of such a wonderful bunch, looks-wise, of course. As for new members of the team, then my mum and dad are on trial.

TMS: And while on teammates, who throws the biggest strop when they are out for a low score?

RC: Not happened yet, but Will Porterfield is ready to go on a mad killing spree the way he storms through the dressing room doors.

TMS: And who is the worst dancer at Warwickshire?

RC: One hundred per cent it has to be Steffan Piolet. He looks like he has iPod headphones in his ears listening to something completely different. He just doesn't know the meaning of the word rhythm.

TMS: And who would be the thickest cricketer you have met?

RC: Ateeq Javid isn't that sharp. Someone asked about a sandwich he was eating, 'Is that fish?' His reply was, 'No, it's tuna'!

TMS: Who is the quickest you have ever faced?

RC: Shoaib Akhtar was wheels and didn't even see it. Nearly rearranged the face of a good-looking lad like myself when I faced him. Maybe, I should have got in the way of it in hindsight?

TMS: Who likes a beer and who falls over after a couple?

RC: Stef Piolet is the biggest lightweight ever. Give him one cider and he is anyone's. Male or female.

TMS: Who else has good banter on the circuit?

RC: Cricketers in general have good banter but Swanny is a hero when it comes to the funnies. I taught him everything he knows.

TMS: Onto secondary cricket matters now, it's going well at Warwickshire isn't it?

RC: Is it? Haven't noticed if I am honest. But seriously, yeah we are going well and enjoy each other's success and have a great team spirit.

TMS: Are we going to see you return to England? You can't be a million miles off given some of the performances recently?

RC: Hopefully I'll keep doing what I have been doing and if I get an opportunity I will obviously not say no. It just goes back to performing for Warwickshire still.

TMS: Why were you batting at nine when you got the ton last year? That's way too low.

RC: We had Trotty and Belly back and with a nightwatchman going in as well, I found myself at nine. I'm back up the order now, though.

TMS: Best food on the circuit?

RC: Lord's is the go-to answer, but haven't been there in a while so I am going to say joint decision with Liverpool and Durham. A great spread.

TMS: What were you taught about sun exposure as a cricketer in your younger days?

RC: Basically to always wear suncream and a hat and to make sure I stayed hydrated. You can even burn through clouds.

TMS: Have you heard of the charity Factor 50 and what are your thoughts on them and the work they do?

RC: I've only heard a bit through Twitter but will definitely have a look in more depth to what they do after finishing this Q & A.

TMS: Who are your best three youngsters coming through in the country?

RC: Laurie Evans of Warwickshire. A seriously talented batter who has the capability to play for England. Tom Milnes at Warwickshire, who is a very talented all-rounder and Sam Billings of Kent, a very organised batter and obviously being looked after well by Rob Key.

TMS: What does the next year hold for you? Being a big Spurs fan, do you fancy being Spurs manager in the future?

RC: That is the million-dollar question. Hopefully keep my form up and maybe get an England tour? If not, then up the Lane to watch Spurs. Not from the bench though, as much as I would love that.

Thanks Rikki, you're a top sport and all of us at The Middle Stump would love to see you return to the England side.

MORE CRICKET UGLIES

The Middle Stump is causing banter all over cricketing changing rooms throughout the country. Our Ugly XI caused merriment, mirth and created ire for those named in the team. We have been sent lots of replies since by club players and professionals, and here are the current heartbreakers currently plying their trade in the county game. Some are harsh, but these are the guys voted for by you ...

SIMON KERRIGAN
Even Cillit wouldn't bang this bloke according to our sources!

SAJ MAHMOOD
I've seen better faces on a Rubik cube!

GARRY PARK
So ugly, he is known to even spike his own drink!

JON LEWIS
Allegedly when he was a baby, he had a tinted incubator.

DAVID MASTERS
The wind must have changed when this lad was a kid!

LUKE PROCTOR
So ugly he has to sneak up to his mirror.

REECE TOPLEY
Responsible for the increase in balaclavas throughout Essex.

AZEEM RAFIQ
When naked, people mentally dress him.

MICHAEL BATES
So rough, he couldn't coax Quasimodo out of a burning shed.

JAMES TAYLOR
Known to be an aspiring model. Of burqas.

GARETH BERG: THE ICEMAN COMETH

Gareth Berg is a man who has grabbed his chance with both hands. Having arrived in the UK and played at the same ground as the boys from The Middle Stump, he kept at it, working hard in the Herts League, and was rewarded with a contract with Middlesex. He was then ruled out of most of 2011 with a finger injury before wrapping up promotion with a 130 and a sixfer. Having been tipped for relegation by many pundits, Gareth has been an integral part of the attack that surprised so many people last season, although not us, as Middlesex easily stayed up and at one point were even in with a shout of the championship itself. Here Gareth talks to us about Tim Murtagh's pants and why he is halfway to being a real man and lots more ...

TMS: Was it more of an honour being asked to do the Q & A for us, or be present at the Southgate Adelaide CC (the home club of the boys at The Middle Stump) club dinner last year?

GB: The dinner was a great pleasure for me, and I was overwhelmed by the warm welcome, and seeing a few old faces from years ago. I always have a soft spot for the club. As for being asked to do a Q &A, always an honour, there's some funny bits in here ...

TMS: What is your nickname and where does it originate from?

GB: Bergy has always been stuck with me since I was a nipper, my mother used to, and still does call me Iceman.

TMS: Who on the county circuit can drink the most beers? And who can put away the least?

GB: Well I've certainly eased off the drink, as it takes ages to recover now. My days over at the Southgate bar and stumbling over to my couch in the groundsman's shed are over ... ah, the good days when you drink hard and have a rubbish season as a pro! Do they still have those leather sofas in the Adelaide? Plenty of booze and pizza spilt on there!

TMS: Unfortunately with other things spilt on there that didn't wipe off so easily, if you get my drift, we removed the sofa. We do have a lovely lemon three-piece suite in there now though. Come and see it next time you're in N14?

TMS: Who is the best-dressed, and who is the worst?

GB: Certainly Finny is up there, although if I had that amount of money I couldn't go wrong. As for the worst attire, then Murtagh is up there with tight XS women's shirts on trying to make himself look super strong and some of the most outrageous boxers! Money well wasted. Mind you, he managed to get the lovely Karina to marry him though.

TMS: You've played for Italy in the past haven't you, such as the ICC Tournament before the start of the 2012 season? Where has the Italian connection come from? I believe you had quite a decent tournament?

GB: Ha, well it comes from my mother's father, and I was quite lucky, I suppose. I have never even been to Italy but I eat the world's largest amount of pizza and love Italian cars, so I guess it's in the blood.

TMS: What are the chances of an England call-up over the next year or so?

GB: No chance! I'm not fussed on that, my priority is with Middlesex first and foremost. If something ever came from that, who knows?

TMS: Tea is an extremely important part of the game. Where are the best teas on the circuit?

GB: Radlett CC have extremely delicious teas … as for county level, I have to say Lord's – nothing beats it.

TMS: Best sledge you have dished out? Best sledge received?

GB: For some reason I don't tend to get any sledging, but one I do hear when playing Kent, is that Rob Key always calls me a clubbie! As for sledging myself … I don't partake, I prefer to talk with the ball.

TMS: Who is the quickest bowler you have faced? Have you ever literally been bricking it as someone has run into bowl?

GB: Chris Tremlett two years ago at Lord's; he bowled a spell up there with the fastest and most skilful I've had to endure. He went on to take a fivefer, I think, with the new ball, almost taking my head off. I have memories of a fizzing seam flying past my lid!

TMS: Favourite ground to play on?

GB: Lord's by far, but one of my favourites would have to be Hove, as it reminds me of Cape Town with the smell of the sea and the seagulls overhead.

TMS: Ever played with a hangover?

GB: Sadly yes, and never again. I was in overnight, and put it this way, facing someone who bowls at 85mph when you are still tipsy is life-threatening! I didn't last more than six balls the following day.

TMS: Name three of the best up-and-coming youngsters in the English system?

GB: Sam Robson, old school, grinding it out and spending all day at the crease type of batsman. Also Ravi Patel, who is a stylish left-arm spinner with great skills and lots of attitude and Tom Helm, an up-and-coming seamer. Watch this space.

TMS: Where is the best curry house in the UK?

GB: The Laguna in Ealing.

TMS: Which of your teammates goes big and likes a vindaloo, and who wimps out with a korma?

GB: Don Shelley, scorer for us at Middlesex, eats vindaloo with ease. I'm a Madras lover, so halfway to being a real man. Tim Murtagh and Dexy (Neil Dexter) are softies: it's korma all the way for them.

TMS: Your career in England started at the Walker Ground in Southgate. What are your views on the ground?

GB: Lovely picturesque ground, I have fond memories of playing there, and working there as a groundsman opened my eyes to county cricket, as Middlesex played there.

TMS: Is it true that Middlesex turned up when you were playing for Radlett to have a look at Kabir Toor, then you had a blinder and they offered you a contract?

GB: Well to be honest, I have no idea exactly. All I know is my name flew about at a time Chad Keegan and JD (Jamie Dalrymple) were leaving the club, so they were in need of an all-rounder. I was offered a lifeline by John Emburey and I was very lucky I guess.

TMS: Did you think your chance of playing as a professional had gone?

GB: All I could do was my best in the leagues and life sorts itself out. I guess it did in this case. Never give up the dream; it took me ten years from leaving school to getting to play my first first-class game!

TMS: How do you think the county game will go? Do you think there will be more T20? What are your views on the County Championship?

GB: I'm a massive fan of four-day cricket; T20 is fun and happy-go-lucky cricket for the *hoi polloi*, but I'm excited to get back to championship stuff. That will never die out.

TMS: Talk us through your finger injury back in 2011? What happened? Pretty horrific, wasn't it, with a snapped tendon?

GB: Simple diving catch at second slip, I snapped my finger back and it was put back into place. Afterwards, though, there was no movement in the last knuckle which led to the suspicion that all was not well. Therefore, surgery was needed to reattach the tendons that were snapped from the bone. It was a needless injury at a time I definitely did not need it. I am still told by Ant Ireland that I dropped it. What the fuck?

TMS: A sixfer and a cheeky little 130-odd from you when you came back from injury saw the boys to the title in Div 2 in 2011. How long did the celebrations go on for, and where?

GB: Wow, that was one of the highlights of my short career thus far. It was an awesome feeling to contribute to the team after they did so well the whole season. It was in Leicester and the party went on until the sun came up! Why not, eh? Plenty of booze and plenty of fun!

TMS: What were you taught about sun protection when you were young? Especially growing up in South Africa.

GB: Always to put some on in any conditions. In South Africa it is one of the harshest environments for sunburn, so even when it feels like there's no chance of burning, always to put some on.

TMS: Also, have you heard of the charity Factor 50? And what do you think of the work they do?

GB: Yes a little bit. It is vitally important to make people aware of the dangers of skin cancer, and the easy ways to prevent it when out

in the sun. As cricketers, it's our role to show people how to do it and to let children who spend time outdoors playing sports know that a cap and sunscreen is a MUST! They do a great job.

TMS: What does the next year hold for you?

GB: I'm hoping for a complete year of cricket to show off some skills and obviously help my team do the best we can. And of course I'm excited to be part of our new charity we have taken on, that charity being Shooting Stars. It's a local charity, close to our hearts.

TMS: Gareth, thank you for your time, you've been an absolute legend and we'll have a drink next time you are back in Southgate. Best of luck to you and all the boys at Middlesex this year.

WHY I LOVE MIDDLESEX

Wayne Wendell Daniel. Three words and one huge man encapsulate why I love Middlesex. This cricket-mad eight-year-old was taken to Lord's back in the late 1970s for the first time and fell in love with the place, the occasion, the history and much more, but it was asking the Bajan opening bowler for his autograph that made me worship the man, and the team in general.

The man known as Diamond was on his way back from the Nursery End nets, and dropped all of his gear to sign an autograph for me. Not only that, he asked me for my name, and when I replied 'Daniel, he responded with 'Dat's my name too!' before patting one very proud North London child on the head and signing.

Of course Middlesex at the time had many other great players, and were one of the most successful sides in the country, all of which helped to cement my support of them.

The spin twins Philippe Henri Edmonds and John Ernest Emburey were two of the finest slow bowlers of their time, often bowling in tandem for their country as well as their county. They were diverse in character, one a South London boy from Peckham, and the other being educated at Cambridge. They are however, responsible for two of the more amusing cricketing quotes.

Edmonds, having had a long tour of India, was asked by a journalist what he was looking forward to most on his return to England. He responded with, 'A dry fart!' Emburey, meanwhile, was asked once how his aging back was, and retorted, 'The fackin' fucker's fackin' fucked'.

Edmonds also managed to get himself into hot water in India on a later tour by a form of protest at the slow scoring of Dilip Vengsarkar, and by his frustration at the umpteenth match descending into a draw on the slow, subcontinental featherbeds. While fielding at square leg, Edmonds produced a copy of the *Daily Telegraph* and proceeded to read it, at one point even attempting to do the crossword. The stuff of legends unless you were his skipper!

Opening the bowling they had Wayne Daniel, always bowling with the wind. Every county in the 1970s, apart from Yorkshire, seemed to have a West Indian quick – Holding, Garner, Croft, Marshall, Roberts – all played here and even their reserve attack had more than handy guys like Sylvester Clarke terrifying batsmen at The Oval, or Hallam Moseley at Somerset, a man who would underarm the ball in 90 yards from the boundary. It goes to show the strength in depth that the Windies had at the time, as Wayne played only a handful of matches for them.

At the other end was Mike Selvey, a man who was forced to do the graft, and of whom Mike Brearley quoted, 'Because I used to use him bowling into the wind, his nose got flatter and flatter every season.' Selvey is now one of the finest cricket journalists around, writing for the *Guardian*, and is someone known to have the occasional read of The Middle Stump, which as you know, must make you an erudite individual! Another man who bowled a lot back then, before too many Lord's lunches turned him into a specialist batsman, was Mike Gatting.

The batting department had Gatting himself, one of the best young players in England at the time, and a man who would go on to lead his country, the lovable Wilf Slack who, sadly is no longer with us, as well as that thief of runs, Clive Radley. Radley would nudge, nurdle and turn ones into twos, and always produced on the big one-day stage. The line-up at various times included the fine left-hander Graham Barlow, the hard-hitting Roland Butcher, and Norman Featherstone, who was born in the wonderfully named Que Que.

Leading them all was the finest England captain of all time: Michael Brearley. The man responsible for saving Ian Botham's career, wasn't always popular with his players, as the idiosyncratic Edmonds would often walk backwards to his bowling mark to make sure that Brearley didn't change the field. Brearley, along with Sunil Gavaskar, were the first pioneers of head protection, and according to Selvey, the skullcap that he wore under his hat, was homemade, along with his own hair glued to the sides to make it look like he wasn't wearing protective gear.

Brearley, who it was said by Rodney Hogg had a 'degree in people', wasn't always so popular with all Australians either, a moment defined when Dennis Lillee produced an aluminium bat. Apparently, all of the players knew it was dodgy, and when the first ball was pushed into the covers amid a massive metallic clang, the game was interrupted as Lillee

and Brearley had a stand-up row for twenty minutes, while the other players were rolling around laughing.

A few seasons later other heroes emerged such as Vince van der Bijl, a huge South African, and Norman Cowans. Others were Simon Hughes, now the analyst on TV, Paul Downton and Neil Williams. Jeff Thomson, described by Graeme Fowler in his interview with us as the quickest he has faced, also made a brief appearance for the county in the early 1980s.

Middlesex is a county which has produced many fine cricketers over the years: Ramprakash, Tufnell, Fraser, as well as the current crop which includes Denly, Murtagh, Berg, Simpson, Rogers and Finn, and they are more than capable of continuing this tradition. Still though, the reason I support Middlesex goes back to 1978, and that chance meeting with the big Barbadian, Wayne Daniel.

TOMMY RUNDLERS

The Thorpster gives us his take on those who have picked up most of the wickets in the wet summer of 2012. Those dibbly-dobblies, often entered into the scorebook as T. Rundler, thrived in the wet conditions, much to the chagrin of Thorpster.

In that most miserable of cricketing summers, those miserly exponents of the art of medium swing and seam bowling affectionately known as Tommy Rundlers had a wonderful time across the length and the breadth of the country. These boys like nothing better than opening their curtains on a Saturday morning before the match and rubbing their hands together at the sight of rain falling from the sky.

I have always disliked such bowlers from the point of view of an opening batsman and spectator. As a player, the thought of patting the ball to mid-off and on for 10 overs on a wet wicket was a painful nightmare. With the score at about 16–1 and me on about 4, I would inevitably succumb to a swipe across the line and 9 times out of 10 either hole out, or miss and be lbw or bowled.

As a spectator watching cricket on TV during school holidays in the 1970s and '80s I hated nothing more than watching a county or international game with a Tommy Rundler opening from one end partnered by Sir Wobbly at the other on a wet one. I remember watching in utter boredom as Colin Dredge or Colin Tunnicliffe plodded in with a ring field. At my favourite county, Middlesex, you had Simon Hughes, now an esteemed cricket analyst trundling in, and also back in the day, one of The Middle Stump's heroes, Gatt, lobbing 'em down.

Of course the county game was dominated by Tommys as the soggy conditions dictated. But in those days, the England selectors also had a penchant for picking dull medium-pacers. Those of my vintage will remember Test caps for Arnie Sidebottom (affectionately known as Assie Side Ass by sniggering schoolboys), Neal Radford (the Worcester wobbler), Alan Igglesden (the mulleted, moustachioed one) and Ian Greig (whose only similarity to his brother Tony was the crazy Arthur Scargill-style hair).

I always wanted England to go for the quick men and was delighted when commentators declared the short-lived opening combination of Gladstone Small and Graham Dilley as the quickest combination for a decade.

The type of Tommy I have talked about are OK in English conditions with the ball wobbling in the air like Rik Waller and moving around at a sharper angle than a David Cameron U-turn. However, when faced with conditions other than damp and dank, they struggle big time. Although being slightly quicker than a Tommy, such a fate befell English/Australian 'pace man' Martin McCague. Standing in for the injured genuine pace man Devon Malcolm, the Kent bowler was smashed all over the place, leading to yours truly waking up to headlines of: 'Slater feasts on McCague's diet of half volleys'.

Thankfully England now have an abundance of fast-bowling talent, but not so long ago in a home Ashes series, England opened up with a 'lightning

quick' attack of Martin Bicknell and James 'Chucker' Kirtley steaming in at 73mph. We still see the odd bizarre horses for courses selection, particularly at Headingley, such as Darren 'the Aussie roof tiler' Pattinson, whose brother James now chucks them down for the auld enemy.

So to me, the choice between watching a quick steaming in with a new red cherry with an attacking field or a mystery spinner with men round the bat, as opposed to Jeremy Coney or Chris Harris wobbling it down with a ring field, is an easy one to make.

Roll on the great British summer, and the hardening and cracking of tracks, creating the type of crazy-paving-type surface which turns Dominic Littlewood incandescent with rage on *Cowboy Builders*.

A DAY IN THE FIELD: MARK FIELD MP

The Middle Stump spoke to cricket-loving MP for the Cities of London and Westminster, Mark Field. A new fan of our site, Mark has had a lifelong interest in the game, and talks to us about Essex winning the Benson & Hedges Cup in 1979, his views on cricket and which politicians would make good players.

Elected as an MP in 2001, Mark has been returned to Parliament with an increased majority at every election since, and the ex-small businessman has a keen interest in most sports. He is the Vice Chairman of the All Party Parliamentary Group on Football, among other things, but we spoke to him about another of his loves, cricket.

TMS: Mark, it must be an absolute privilege being asked by such a classy publication as The Middle Stump to do a Q & A with us?

MF: Always a pleasure – and an honour too!

TMS: What do you think of the blog so far?

MF: Clearly a lot of work has gone into it and I love the mischievous nature of the interviews. Cricket is often perceived by the uninitiated as a slow game appealing only to older men, but this work will certainly appeal to a younger audience far more than your more traditional cricketing reporting.

TMS: When did you first get into cricket?

MF: I was first introduced to cricket when I started primary school as my father played for a local club, Tring Park CC. I immediately loved it! I found that I was somewhat better suited to cricket than my other sporting passion, football.

TMS: Do you still manage to get to any games?

MF: Unfortunately I do not get to see as much cricket as I might like. As a father of two pre-school children and an MP, my evenings and weekends are usually pretty hectic. I don't often get to see my county team, Essex, play.

TMS: Who are your current favourite players?

MF: Alastair Cook – a solid opening bat who plays exactly like I would have loved to and he's an Essex man to boot.

TMS: Do you think English cricket is in a good place at present?

MF: English cricket has come a tremendously long way since the introduction of promotion and relegation to the County Championship in 2000. A whole new generation has come through since then and we are (for now at least) the best Test side in the world and current T20 World Champions. With the young talent coming through – Jonny Bairstow, Jos Buttler and Stuart Meaker – English cricket is in a good place for the foreseeable future. It is also pleasing to see the women's team doing fantastically well having won the World Cup and World T20 competition recently.

TMS: You play for the Commons cricket team, don't you? Who else is into their cricket from the House? Do you bat or bowl?

MF: I'm afraid I'm a bit old for all that now. I used to be a batsman and in fact opened the batting for Berkshire under-12s while at school with the ex-Barnet and current Gillingham football manager, Martin Allen.

TMS: Dennis Skinner looks like he would be an opposition quick with a sledge or two up his sleeve, while Ed Balls is maybe a nagging, annoying seamer who you struggle to get away. Which other MPs would you have analogies of, cricket-wise?

MF: I suppose Nick Clegg would make the ideal twelfth man. Following a flurry of wickets towards the close of play, Michael Fallon would be the man you'd call upon to steady the ship as the reliable nightwatchman. Nadine Dorries may not be subtle enough to bowl a googly or a doosra, but would be effective nonetheless.

TMS: There is a generation of English kids growing up who don't get to see the game as it is no longer broadcast on terrestrial TV. What are your views on this? Or do you think Sky's money coming into the game has made it more professional, shall we say, much in the way it improved football?

MF: It is a great shame there isn't more sport in general on terrestrial TV. The deal with Sky has allowed far more cricket to be shown on TV and in fairness encouraged cricket to modernise and

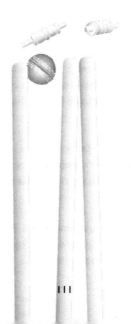

brand itself more effectively. The level of technological innovation has been fantastic! Far more damaging to cricket, in my opinion, is the lack of it in our state schools and I know this is a trend the ECB has invested a lot of money in reversing.

TMS: Are you a Lancashire man then as well as being a Bury fan?

MF: Curiously I'm a non-Lancastrian Bury supporter. I was actually brought up in Berkshire but given their minor county status I've always been an Essex fan, and was there at Lord's in 1979 when they won their first ever trophy, the Benson & Hedges Cup. Graham Gooch scored 120 and Ken McEwan 70-odd – wonderful memories!

TMS: Who are your favourite top three players of all time?

MF: Ian Botham (truly an all-time great – look at the stats!), Alastair Cook and Barry Richards.

TMS: Ever had too much to drink after a day at the cricket, unlike we ever do here at The Middle Stump?

MF: No comment – now where are my house keys?

TMS: What are your plans for the future and will you get to any games this year, with your hectic schedule?

MF: I've been fortunate enough to be invited to a day at the Lord's and Oval Tests this year, and I very much hope to get myself to some T20 county cricket one evening (if the whips allow me to get away from the House!).

Mark, thank you very much for your time. It is great to speak with cricket-loving, and sport-loving people in general, and we'll buy you a beer if we bump into you at the cricket this year. We'll even find your house keys for you!

So there you go. Mark obviously knows his stuff when it comes to the game, and you could tell he is a real cricket fan, and a man who has followed the sport since he was a young lad.

ENGLAND'S WORST XI

Here we look at the worst players to ever play for England and we wonder if this lot would give Zimbabwe a decent game? Funny how many of them came from the 1980s, isn't it? Let us know on Twitter @themiddlestump who your worst England XI would be.

CHRIS COWDREY (captain)
Amazingly Cowdrey was picked to replace Botham on England's tour of India in 1984, and was one of our famous four skippers in the 1988 season versus the West Indies. Micky Stewart urged him to pull out of the last Test when he was 50/50, then wasn't ever picked again. The son of England legend Colin (see where I'm going here) amassed a massive 101 runs in six matches.

AFTAB HABIB
After averaging 50 in 1998, the Leicestershire batsmen was picked to take on that fearsome, famous bowling attack of New Zealand, post-Hadlee. However, in typical England style he was discarded after two Tests, as the likes of Scott Styris and Darryl Tuffey proved too much for him, and he finished with a Test average of 8.66.

PAUL PARKER
A brilliant fielder, but was picked to replace the out-of-form David Gower at The Oval in 1981. WHAT?!?!? With a big hairdo, Parker contributed a huge 13 runs in his two knocks before being permanently discarded back to Hove, where he eventually captained Sussex.

GRAHAM BARLOW

Unlike me to put a Middlesex man in here, I know, but the opener played Test cricket on the tour of India in '76/'77 and a solitary Test against the Aussies in '77 before the selectors ran out of patience with him. Barlow played three Tests, and in five innings never made it into double figures. He averaged 4.25 with a highest score of a whopping 7 not out!

PAUL TERRY

Vivian Paul Terry, the man with three Christian names, was drafted into the England side during the Blackwash series of 1984. Maybe his Christian name persuaded the old TCCB that he was England's answer to the West Indian Richards, but Winston Davis put us all out of our misery when he broke his arm, and we never saw him again at Test level. Fair play to him though, he did come out to bat with a broken arm, so Allan Lamb could reach his hundred.

IAN GREIG

Tony's little brother took on the might of the Pakistani tourists in 1982 when Derek Pringle got injured, but failed miserably, averaging 6.5 with the bat. He was given two Tests before disappearing into obscurity with Surrey. He went to the same hairdresser as Arthur Scargill.

RICHARD BLAKEY (wicketkeeper)

Our keeper in the side was England's gloveman in the 1993 tour of India, where we lost 3–0. The Yorkshire stumper played in two of those, where England lost by an innings. They always like to say a good keeper should contribute with the bat, and Blakey provided a huge 7 runs in these Tests, at an average of 1.75. Maybe his namesake from *On the Buses* could have done better?

TONY PIGOTT

England were in New Zealand in 1982, and Pigott was out there playing a bit of club cricket and about to get married, when he got the nod on the morning of the game. Pigott must have picked a winning raffle ticket or the England selectors were taking the piss, as they lost by a mere innings and 175 runs! Yes, to the might of New Zealand.

IAN SALISBURY

Scoring 1–193 against the Pakistanis and England's answer to Shane Warne ended up back playing at Surrey. Always reliable, that is if you wanted a full toss or long hop in the over, Salisbury finished with a Test bowling average at just a shade under 77!

MARTIN MCCAGUE

Quick, but lacking in control, this Northern Irish man arrived in the England team via his native Australia. The Aussie press weren't overly happy with him touring their country with England, but they should have been as he was absolutely taken to the cleaners. However, we like McCague as he is rumoured to have downed 72 pints of Guinness on a stag weekend to Dublin, according to Steve Waugh.

DARREN PATTINSON

Another Aussie (via Grimsby) who played for England. England's selectors went back to their 1980s policy when this guy was drafted in relatively recently. No less a judge than Sir Ian Botham described it as 'the most idiological, pathetic and diabolical piece of selecting I have ever seen', as he was picked in place of Steve Harmison. Unsurprisingly, that was Pattinson's only Test.

ANDY NASH: THE CIDERMAN

At The Middle Stump we like cricket people. We pride ourselves on being cricket people, writing a blog *for* cricket people. So when we caught up with Somerset CCC chairman, Andy Nash, it was an absolute pleasure, and we got the sense he'd be as happy chipping in at his local village club as he would being the driving force behind arguably, the most successful county in the country over the last few years.

Here Andy gives us the lowdown on cider, T20, overseas players and the success of those boys down in the Wild West, and you can feel his passion for the club. Not sure about Trescothick being an up-and-coming young player though, Andy!

TMS: It must be a huge privilege doing a Q & A with The Middle Stump. Are you enjoying our stuff so far?

AN: It's a pleasure. And so is your work.

TMS: Things seem to be going down well in the West Country? Who likes their cider the best out of the Somerset players? And is Thatcher's still the best stuff? Comes from Sandford, I believe?

AN: We are known as the Cidermen, of course. The players are very fond of Thatcher's and when in India for the CLT20 we suffered withdrawal symptoms and requested supplies to be shipped out. I've little doubt this wonderful cider and its proven beneficial effects (an apple a day …) are the secret behind our phenomenal run to the semi-final!

TMS: How was the Champions League T20 Trophy in 2011? You got to the semi-final, didn't you?

AN: It was a terrific experience and reminded us all of how unpredictable cricket can be. We arrived knackered from a Lord's final, minus our captain, without a regular wicketkeeper and proceeded to dispatch all comers until we met the eventual winners Mumbai Indians in the semi-final … and we would have won that if Buttler hadn't poleaxed Kieswetter with a vicious on-drive!

The Indians love their cricket, but received our very loud renditions of the Blackbird song after each victory with a mixture of bemusement and terror.

TMS: Do you think T20 will take over from the four-day game?

AN: No, I don't believe that any more than I believe rock music will kill off classical music. There's room for both and we should celebrate the fact we've discovered a new format which so many fans enjoy.

TMS: What is your view on players playing it ahead of playing for their country such as certain West Indians did last year?

AN: I think that's entirely a matter for the individual players. One volunteer is better than ten pressed men!

TMS: Is it ruining the domestic game in certain countries, where players don't play for their own counties, preferring to take the rupees of the IPL?

AN: T20 is now widely accredited as having improved key cricketing skills ... fielding and slow bouncers being just two examples. Also teams will now set about chasing 200 or more in the last session to win a County Championship match. Unheard of before T20.

TMS: Somerset showed a profit of £408,000 last year. What is the secret to your success?

AN: Obviously it's a secret and I can't tell you! We are a members club and we own our ground so we have no shareholders to pay, nor ground rent to find. Also, with our new catering, events and retail assets, we have built a substantial income outside of cricket. The County Ground used to be busy for 40 days a year – now it's busy for 340 days.

TMS: Do you miss the halcyon days of Somerset in the '70s and '80s when Garner, Richards and Botham ruled the roost?

AN: Of course – who wouldn't? But we are in another golden period and have the most terrifically talented young squad who will help keep us at the top of the game in England … and win trophies.

TMS: How long did you have Vernon Philander?

AN: He left us in the second half of May.

TMS: And what's your view of people saying that offering him an opportunity to get used to English conditions hurt the England side later in the year?

AN: I am a cricket fan first and foremost and cricketers of the calibre of Vernon Philander would grace any cricket pitch and richly entertain all supporters lucky enough to see him play. Players of his standing should be welcome anywhere and anytime. It's true, he learnt about bowling in English conditions, but also the England batters got to know more about him. Lastly, Team England will have wanted to play and beat the best team SA can muster – not one that had been unfairly deprived of the best possible preparation.

TMS: At The Middle Stump, we have always been told by the ladies that it is best to come second. Are you tired of Somerset coming second all the time, and will that change this year?

AN: I'd suggest it's better to come second than to miss out on the experience completely. I think everyone will be delighted should we come first now and again.

TMS: When are you going to get the Giles Clarke job? Is being Somerset Chairman the warm-up job for the ECB role? A bit like a Yorkshire fast bowler in previous years would open the bowling for England?

AN: It is a great privilege to chair a famous club like Somerset and my priority is to continue to lead the club towards better things. Since 2004 we have completed three of the four phases of the redevelopment of the County Ground – we now need to complete the final phase. We are also been working towards gaining

Category B status for the County Ground which if granted will bring ODIs and International T20s to the West Country. There can be no greater prize than that! Once we've a achieved that, and we will, it would be for others to decide whether I can serve the game at a higher level.

TMS: Who are your best three young cricketers in the country?

AN: Craig Kieswetter, Jos Buttler and Marcus Trescothick.

TMS: Best bar at a cricket ground in the country?

AN: The Taunton Long Room.

TMS: Favourite ground other than Taunton?

AN: West Bagborough CC.

TMS: What are your plans for the next year?

AN: Silverware, achieve Category B status, make further progress towards the final phase of development of the County Ground and to lead the Somerset Chairman's XI to victory over John Gannon's eCar side.

Andy, thanks for the interview with The Middle Stump, and we wish you, and Somerset, all the best for the coming season.

CRICKET FATTIES XI

Cricket has always been a game that has attracted the more rotund types. Many players at club level have overcome anorexia, but here The Middle Stump looks at the tubbies who have made it further up the cricketing, erm, food chain. Here we pick our best eleven cricketing fatties.

WARWICK ARMSTRONG – Described by *Sporting Life* as 'rather like a fat uncle, not altogether unlike a fat aunt', the 22-stone Australian is the heaviest man known to have played Test cricket. On a tour to England he was once followed around by a young chap in a match at Southampton. Eventually the tubby Victorian offered to sign the boy's autograph book before getting the reply of 'No thanks sir, you are the only decent bit of shade in the place!'

INZAMAM-UL-HAQ – The Podge from the Punjab was run out over forty times in one-day cricket. However, the incident that really brought him fame was when he was subjected to being called 'aloo' (meaning potato) by some comedian with a megaphone in Canada in 1997. England spinning coach Mushtaq Ahmed, the Pakistani twelfth man, brought out a bat, which Inzy took from him before proceeding to kick the living daylights out of the bloke in the crowd. Do NOT call him a potato on any account.

ARJUNA RANATUNGA – The Colossus from Colombo was once denied a runner by the Australians. Claiming he had sprained something or other, Ian Healy told him that 'you don't get a runner for being an overweight, unfit, fat c**t'. Unfortunately for the Aussie keeper this was picked up on the stump microphone and broadcast live to millions watching on Aussie TV. Ranatunga refused to shake hands afterwards with the Aussies, while Healy became a legend to millions of kids watching!

DWAYNE LEVEROCK – The Bermudan behemoth and star of the 2007 World Cup attracted headlines such as 'Bermuda Pie-angle' and 'Lard before wicket' as he played England in a warm-up game, picking up a handy couple of wickets with his left-arm spin. The policeman took a stunning, one-handed, diving slip catch in that World Cup against

India but rumours of this causing subsequent earthquakes and tsunamis around the Caribbean are unfounded.

COLIN MILBURN – Nicknamed Ollie in reference to him looking like Oliver Hardy, Milburn was a brilliant batsman and fielder who sadly lost his eye in a car crash at the age of twenty-seven. Milburn's weight was down to his fondness for beer, and was advised to order just half-pints by the England management on a tour in an effort to try to get him fitter. Ollie's response? 'Well I'll just have two halves then, please.' Legend!

ANDY MOLES – The Warwickshire opening bat was known to have had a plate of sandwiches brought to him at the crease which, despite the jeering of the crowd, was to boost his blood sugar levels, he having been diagnosed with diabetes. Later became the New Zealand coach but resigned after disagreements with his players. Maybe they ate all the cake at tea?

JESSE RYDER – The Kiwi was described by Adam Parore as 'too fat and in no fit state to play for New Zealand'. Ryder's season came to an abrupt end in 2007 when he punched a bar window trying to break in at 5.30 one morning, lacerating all the tendons in his hand. Whether he was after the beer or the bar snacks is still a mystery. It was announced in March 2012 that he was taking a break from all cricket, but just a month later he appeared in the IPL. Well, they do have good food in India!

BARRY JARMAN – When the ex-Aussie keeper walked up the stairs it was like the end of *EastEnders*. He was known for his stamina after keeping in the hot sun, although we think the only pain barrier he went through was pain au chocolat! After becoming a match referee, rumours that he and Bruce Reid went to a fancy dress party as the number 10 are unfounded.

MERV HUGHES – Allegedly, when asked by a dietician what he would be eating that night, the moustachioed Victorian replied by saying, 'Pizza'. Concerned, she then said, 'That's OK, but how many slices will you be having?' Merv chortled, 'Depends how many they cut it up into!' Another legendary story was when a fellow fatty of the female variety approached him on the tour to England in 1989. Apparently she approached him nervously saying, 'Sorry, I'm not very good at breaking the ice,' to which he replied, 'Have yer tried jumping?'

JACK SIMMONS – The Lancastrian legend was known for his fondness of fish and chips. Once told Graeme Fowler to stop his car outside the fish and chip shop in Accrington and when he returned, Foxy turned the key in the engine. 'Where in the bloody hell do you think you're going?' asked Simmons. 'Errr, taking you home!' came the reply. Simmons responded with 'Don't do that or the wife won't make me dinner when I get in'. Simmons was known to have wolfed four portions of fish and chips at one sitting.

SAMIT PATEL – The Nottinghamshire spinner is one of the few current players to make our team, which is a sad indictment as to what cricket has become. Left out of the England one-day side owing to his weight problems, he has recently returned. Samit is known to be environmentally friendly and has an energy-saving lightbulb in his fridge.

MIKE GATTING

With over 60,000 runs in first-class cricket and 79 England Test appearances under his belt, we were incredibly privileged to speak to Mike Gatting. A former England captain, he is one of the few English skippers to win a series out in Australia (in 1986/87), and holds the record for the highest score by an Englishman in India. Now Managing Director of the ECB's Cricket Partnerships, Gatt gives us the lowdown on Phil Tufnell, Mike Brearley and answers the usual Middle Stump questions.

TMS: Mike, firstly thank you for agreeing to speak with us. It must be a huge privilege to be interviewed by such a classy bunch as The Middle Stump?

MG: Without a doubt …

TMS: What are you up to these days?

MG: I'm the Managing Director of Cricket Partnerships for the ECB. We oversee all recreational cricket, such as clubs, schools, women, disabled cricket and I have a team of boys and girls working for me here. We also oversee Sport England, and I look after the first-class game with Alan Fordham, the ex-Northamptonshire player.

TMS: Who was the quickest you ever faced?

MG: Three times I have been in the line of fire. Michael Holding in 1981 in Barbados bowled really quick. Sylvester Clarke for Surrey against Middlesex on a quick deck at The Oval once, and Allan Donald at Edgbaston was the other. It was just after that famous incident there, where a pitched-up ball went over Athers' head for four byes over the keeper, and we were fortunate enough to play on the same pitch a few days later!

TMS: Is it true you once took Phil Tufnell for a haircut?

MG: I don't remember that, but I certainly told him to get his hair cut otherwise he wouldn't be coming back.

TMS: Who could drink the most back in your day? We've heard stories about certain players like Frank Hayes having sixteen pints a night?

MG: Frank Hayes was certainly an interesting character! Sixteen pints would have been a good starter for that lot up there back then. I personally never lasted that long. Three or four was my limit. My roommate, Ian 'Gunner' Gould didn't do too badly in that respect. Towards the end we preferred to drink wine rather than beer. We got snobby towards the end!

TMS: And the least?

MG: Not sure really. You'd get guys who would drink halves of bitter while others drank pints, but no one really fell over.

TMS: Who would throw the worst strop when they were out for a duck?

MG: Mark Ramprakash. Let's say he was rather passionate about the game, and when he got out he was upset. Although saying that, we all got wound up when we were out. I was no stranger to it, and was involved in an incident myself where I broke a pane of glass at Lord's. I pushed the door too hard!

TMS: So Matt Prior was just trying to emulate you then?

MG: Haha! I'm not too sure about that!

TMS: Who was the maddest you played with and against?

MG: All of Essex were lunatics apart from Gooch and Fletcher. Some of the pranks people like Ray East and John Lever got up to were unbelievable, but they were a great bunch of lads. Derek Randall would have to be the maddest I played with. He lived in a dream world. Saying that, he was a superb cricketer – a good bat and a brilliant fielder. He used to practice catching skiers behind his back. If you or I tried that it would hit us on the head, yet Randall would catch them every time.

TMS: What about David Smith at Surrey?

MG: He was a gentle giant really. He had this persona of being aggressive on the pitch and I suppose it did intimidate some players, but he was OK.

TMS: Who was the worst dressed?

MG: Philip Tufnell, closely followed by a certain Mr Michael Brearley. Brears used to arrive in the changing room in these Indian garments. Selve – Mike Selvey – was another. He would wear these scruffy t-shirts in the 1970s with 'No Wucking Furries' written across them, which has to be said, didn't exactly impress the MCC members.

TMS: What were you taught about sun protection when you were younger?

MG: Luckily my parents were very good in that respect. We'd generally put on suncream, although occasionally we got a reminder and we'd have to sleep with calamine lotion on our backs. As players we knew, but we didn't do it all the time. When we went to really hot places like India, Sri Lanka or the West Indies, we'd slap it on.

TMS: What do you think of Factor 50 and the work they do?

MG: I think they do a brilliant job. With the hole in the ozone layer getting bigger and more harmful radiation, the sun certainly feels a lot stronger these days than it used to. Maybe that is because I am getting older and my skin is more fragile? Skin cancer is horrid. Andy Flower having the melanoma removed is a reminder to us all, and you hear about Aussie cricketers having them removed from their faces, hands and ears, so it is great work that they do.

TMS: Which venue on the circuit serves the best food?

MG: Lord's. You can't beat it upstairs there. Abbeydale in Sheffield was always excellent too. Generally all of them are good now and offer healthier varieties of food. Derby and Leicester were never great back in the day.

TMS: Best three youngsters coming through in the country?

MG: Joe Root, Jonny Bairstow and Steven Finn.

TMS: When we spoke to Ed Giddins he said Finn has the ability to be a 300 Test wicket man at 24 apiece.

MG: I agree with him.

TMS: So when you look back on your career what are the memories? Hopefully not Malcolm Marshall's perfume ball, or Shane Warne's 'ball of the century'?

MG: I would have to say the best experience was the Ashes tour of 1986/87 and winning out there. Although the 1984 trip to India was a great trip, albeit quite a tough one with the assassination of Mrs Gandhi. Adversity abroad and all that!

TMS: Haven't you got the highest score by an Englishman in India, although Fowler held the record for a couple of hours, didn't he, when he got his double hundred first?

MG: Something like that. No, the Aussie tour just pips it, as we were told we were useless and the press slated us. It was the famous 'can't bat, can't bowl, can't field' tour. I remember lots fondly though – being made captain of England, my first game ever at Lord's and bringing up my first hundred for Middlesex. I even remember the shot, which was a sweep off Phil Carrick.

TMS: Mike, it has been a fantastic career and a real pleasure having a chat with you. We'll have a beer in Southgate at some point.

MG: Definitely and thank you.

DIALOGUE WITH DIMI

Dimitri Mascarenhas is a hero to those down in Hampshire. A great all-rounder and a brilliant fielder, he is one of the finest one-day players in recent years. Shane Warne was amazed England hadn't picked him, and when they did, he hit five sixes in an over against India. He has captained Hampshire to Lord's silverware, played in the Champions Trophy in T20 for Otago, and also become a living legend in India during his time with the Rajasthan Royals and Kings XI Punjab. He also led Hampshire to the T20 trophy in 2012.

TMS: Dimi, thanks for agreeing to do the Q & A with The Middle Stump. As a man who has played cricket all over the world and is a legend in numerous countries, it must be a huge privilege to be asked by us?

DM: No problem. It's all good fun and I'm happy to be involved.

TMS: You've recently become a parent, I believe? Getting much sleep?

DM: I'm OK now as he is nine months old, but I wasn't getting too much to start off with.

TMS: Not many people I have spoken to have had Shane Warne at their wedding. Did Liz Hurley catch the bouquet?

DM: Ha. She wasn't in a huge rush to dive for it! That was the first time I met Liz, at my wedding.

TMS: What was it like playing with Warnie? What was his banter like?

DM: He was absolutely brilliant. He came over in 2000 and stayed for about six or seven years in total and he was fantastic. A different class with the ball, and definitely different class with the ability to chat people out. A great man to play with.

TMS: So how did a guy of Sri Lankan heritage, brought up in Australia, with a Russian or Greek Christian name, end up playing for England?

DM: My parents are Sri Lankan although I was born in England. I guess my mum just liked the name.

TMS: Everyone will remember you for slapping Yuvraj Singh (wasn't it?) for five consecutive sixes. What was the buzz of that like, for England in front of a full house?

DM: Yeah it was Yuvraj. Huge, just huge. I walked to the crease and Owais Shah was smashing it around and there were just a few balls left. I was just trying to give him the strike to be honest, and the first ball I coughed to mid-wicket. The boys weren't too happy with it, but as you know, the next five balls are history.

TMS: And then you hit someone in a T20 for four on the bounce, didn't you? Who was the bowler?

DM: Yes, that was Jeetan Patel in New Zealand.

TMS: Which batsman has taken you apart the worst and what were the figures?

DM: Darren Lehmann used to do it regularly. I didn't look at figures! Chris Gayle too. He has hit me for three sixes in an over twice. Once for England and once in the IPL.

TMS: Which of your teammates has pulled the worst bird ever?

DM: Erm … let me have a think. Nope I can't answer that on record!

TMS: Who on the county circuit can drink the most beers? And who can put away the least?

DM: At Hampshire we have a fines system. Danny Briggs is shocking. He gets fined regularly. In fact both he and Michael Bates are rubbish at drinking! As for the most – Durham as a club. All the lads at Durham CCC like a beer.

TMS: Who is the best dressed, and who is the worst?

DM: The young lads like James Vince think they're really cool but they're not. Ervine and Bates would be the worst. Actually stick Vince and Wood in there too. Yeah, Wood definitely.

TMS: Tea is an extremely important part of the game. Where are the best teas on the circuit?

DM: Lord's. By a mile.

TMS: Who throws the worst strop when they're out? Who do you have to go and put a helmet on for just when they come back through the dressing-room door?

DM: Dawson. Watch out when he's out!

TMS: Who is the quickest bowler you have faced? Have you ever literally been bricking it as someone has run into bowl?

DM: Brett Lee and Mitchell Johnson – they were both very fast.

TMS: Favourite ground to play on?

DM: My home ground, the Ageas Bowl, but Lord's is also just a beautiful place to play.

TMS: Ever played with a hangover?

DM: I spent my whole first year with a hangover in 1998!

TMS: Name three of the best up-and-coming youngsters coming through the English system? Paul Nixon in his interview with us was glowing about the praise for Michael Bates as a keeper.

DM: Yeah, he is a great keeper. Maybe his batting is not quite there yet, but he has got his first ton last year. I like Chris Woakes at Warwickshire. With the bat, the ball and in the field, I think he is a future Test star. There are some great youngsters coming through the system – Ben Stokes is another, James Vince, Jos Buttler, Jonny Bairstow – there's a few coming through.

TMS: Have you heard of the charity Factor 50 and what do you think of the work that they do? Were you taught much about sun protection?

DM: Yeah I was taught about it. It's maybe not so much an issue for me, but I am fully aware that I can still get skin cancer. Anyone like them who promotes awareness is doing a good job.

TMS: Best curry house in the UK?

DM: Popadom Express in Oxford Street, Southampton.

TMS: Have you ever played at the Walker Cricket Ground in Southgate, where Middlesex play?

DM: I have. You need your spinners there. Hang on, didn't we get attacked there one year?

TMS: Oh yes, yes you did. A group of local kids bricked the bus on the way out after game, didn't they? I don't think they'd even been to the game. However, I do apologise for your bus getting done – although I didn't personally have any involvement in lobbing the stones!

DM: That's OK mate. I didn't actually play and wasn't there, but the lads told me about it, so yeah we've got really fond memories of playing there!

TMS: How do you think the county game will go? Will there be more T20 and is there still a place for the County Championship?

DM: Of course there is. There is a definite place for the LVCC. There is huge prestige for winning it, and now you have the best teams in Division One. It is a great system. As for T20, now that counties play ten games, they have got it right. The sixteen they played last year was too many. I think the thing needs a revamp – scrap the counties and bring in a franchise system.

TMS: What does the next year hold for you?

DM: You never know what the future holds. I'm still with Hants, but not really sure what is going on regarding the IPL as my deal has come to an end. All I can do is have a good winter and work hard.

TMS: Dimi, thank you very much for your time with The Middle Stump, and hope you get the much-needed sleep!

DM: No worries. A pleasure.

JACK BROOKS

Jack Brooks is like a character from a bygone age. A man who has gone from playing club cricket in Oxfordshire to being on the verge of the England team in four years, he bowls in a headband and is one of the characters of modern-day cricket. No one celebrates a wicket quite like Jack Brooks. We caught up with him before his high-profile move to Yorkshire, while he was injured and not only is he a top bloke, but a bloody funny one at that. With a nickname of SuBo, owing to a resemblance to the Scottish singer, no one deserves success more than this man after all of his hard work, and he is a huge fan of us here at The Middle Stump.

TMS: Jack, thanks for your time. It must be a huge privilege to be asked to be interviewed by such a classy bunch as The Middle Stump?

JB: Massively. It's up there in my career. I can't think of anyone I'd prefer to be interviewed by.

TMS: What do you think of it so far? I see you have read a few of our articles?

JB: Very insightful. It is different from other stuff out there, and the questions are very different from the usual stuff we get asked.

TMS: So you were out injured for a bit of 2012? Not enough of the Old Speckled Hen?

JB: It is definitely not for the lack of the Old Speckled Hen! We were sponsored by them so it was everywhere at Northampton, and we had plenty in our locker. Some of the younger lads aren't that keen on it, so we tended to drink theirs too.

TMS: You must get this question all the time, but you have gone from playing in the Home Counties Premier League to being on the verge of the England side within four years. What advice would you give to someone who is playing a good standard of club cricket who wants to make a career out of the game?

JB: I was told I was never quick enough. I bowled away-swingers with the keeper standing up and maybe didn't take it as seriously as I should have. I was messing about with my mates, but once I decided I was up for it, I knuckled down. I missed the junior systems completely, but I got advice from good people. My advice is to never, ever give up.

TMS: Onto more serious matters now . . . who is the worst dressed at Northants?

JB: Dave Murphy, the keeper, is an interesting character to say the least with his bizarre humour. He is a very special human being, let's say. He wears these tight trousers, and with a typical wicket keeper's large *derrière*, they look they have been sprayed on. Andrew Hall has that classic South African look of jeans with Asics trainers, while Niall O'Brien often can be spotted in a shiny shirt with sequins on!

TMS: Who can drink the most?

JB: David Sales came from a different era. He never shies away from having a drink at the bar or buying a round and Rob Newton has followed him. I like to think I am up there, although the time has to be right. You have to pick and choose your times.

TMS: And the least?

JB: Alex Wakeley. Two pints and he is pissed, but he stays at the same level all night and carries on. He never gets any worse.

TMS: Who is the quickest you have faced?

JB: Dirk Nannes in a T20 a couple of years back, but I would have to say Finn and Meaker are the quickest on the circuit. Meaker bowled me a short one which I backed away from and put him over point for six, so I'll always have that one in my locker. We're good friends actually. Finn is also rapid and has hit me a couple of times. Those two are the quickest in England.

TMS: Who is the worst dancer?

JB: Ben Howgego just doesn't dance. He's my housemate so I know this. His best move is to lean on the bar with a pint in his hand. I'm pretty bad too. I've had some embarrassing moments.

TMS: Who has the worst strop when they are out for a cheap score?

JB: Stephen Peters. He comes in, shuts the door, calmly takes his pads off, puts his bat away in complete silence before going into the shower room and beating the crap out of the walls with various implements. Andrew Hall is another. He puts the bat that he actually bats with away, then takes a special bat out of his locker that he uses for hitting things with! He has a spare bat just to get his frustrations out.

TMS: So you bowl in headband, like digging in the odd short one and follow it up with words. Who else is good for banter?

JB: I don't tend to say too much to be honest, although fast bowlers should have a presence about them, shall we say? Steve Kirby – now he's my cup of tea and a great competitor. I got a fifty against Gloucestershire a couple of years back and he and Jon Lewis abused me virtually every ball. They were telling me to call an ambulance! When it was Kirbs' turn to bat, I told him he was going to get nothing in his own half and let him have a couple of short ones. He was still coming back at me telling me how ugly I was (or words to that effect), but we had a hug and a laugh about it, and made up afterwards.

TMS: So do you sing like Susan Boyle as well as look like her?

JB: Haha brilliant! I wish I did as I would have another career to fall back on. No, I'm the worst singer ever. I'm tone deaf.

TMS: What have you been taught about being exposed to the sun for long periods?

JB: Make sure you slap it on before every session, even when it is cloudy. You just cannot afford to misjudge it, especially abroad in countries like South Africa where there is a bigger hole in the ozone layer. We're out in it all the time so I don't want leathery skin when I'm fifty.

TMS: What do you know about Factor 50 the charity?

JB: They do a fantastic job. It is great that an organisation like them takes notice as cricketers are exposed to it, and the support they offer is brilliant.

TMS: Best three youngsters coming through in the country?

JB: Tymal Mills. I shared a room with him on the England Lions tour last winter in Potch in South Africa, and he is huge. He bowls at 90mph+, and he's my little brother, as big as he is. He is the biggest, strongest bloke I have met and has a huge future ahead of him. Ollie Stone is a lad we have just signed at Northants, who just missed out on the England Under-19s. Another with a bright future. Lastly, David Sales, a resurgent young man with a fine career ahead of him!

TMS: Best food on the circuit?

JB: Only one winner. Lord's. We got 600 there in 2011 over two days, and batting where I do in the order, I spent those two days in my tracksuit. I had a three-course lunch both days and it was top drawer. Derby is also good. We were there first game last year, and the lads were all very impressed.

TMS: What does the future hold for you?

JB: Well, England is the dream, but it is very difficult with five or six very good seamers there, with another five or six of us then competing. We have a great pool of players now, and it will take something special to get in. I just need to keep fit and firing, but I am loving every minute of it. Hopefully I keep improving and can make the EPP squad this winter again.

TMS: What happened to Northants in 2011? A bit of a Devon Loch moment, wasn't it?

JB: Thanks for reminding me. Fair play to Surrey, I think they won four out of four with maximum points to pip us, and they can do that with their brand of cricket. Middlesex and Surrey probably did deserve it.

TMS: We interviewed Gareth Berg the other week, who was a key behind Middlesex going up at the end.

JB: Yeah I played against him when he was at Radlett at club level. He's a great bloke.

TMS: Jack, you've been an absolute superstar and when we come up to Northampton we'll have a couple of Speckled Hens.

JB: No let's have something different. A strawberry daiquiri maybe? The bar staff at Wantage Road won't know what has hit them.

TMS: The strawberry daiquiris are on us!

And with that, Jack went back and worked on getting fit and back in shape for Northamptonshire. Not only a great bowler, but a great bloke too.

COUNTIES

Here at The Middle Stump we give you our latest guide to the counties. We include some information on the counties, along with a brief synopsis of the main ground they play at. Banter Factor will be the member of the county that gives us a few laughs over the years, while something us boys at The Middle Stump are connoisseurs of, which is pubs, also get a mention. Local ales to that part of the world are brought to you by us here, too. Overnight stay factor is whether it is worth a cheeky weekend away, being marked out of ten, while we also discover the local celebrities in that part of the world.

Due to change, some of the information may be out of date by the time you read this, so if it is wrong, then don't blame us but all details were sort of correct in 2013. We take no responsibility if a landlord has changed and the real ale pub we recommend has turned into a blaring music, eighteen-year-old swarming, drug taking, fighting pub and you get a damned good hiding.

Read on and enjoy ...

DERBYSHIRE

Derbyshire County Cricket Club
County Ground
Grandstand Road
Derby
DE21 6AF

Club Colours: Light and Dark Blue

Founded in 1870, Derbyshire were arguably the weakest county during their first fifty years of existence – 1920 saw the club lose every single match! Things started to turn around and the club won their only championship in 1936 with England seamer Bill Copson taking over 100 wickets. In more recent times Derbyshire have been competitive without setting the county scene alight, although they surprisingly won Division Two of the LVCC in 2012. They did, however, also win the Gillette Cup in 1981. Kim Barnett moulded them into a competitive outfit during his tenure of captaincy from 1983 to 1995, bringing success in the form of the Sunday League in 1990 and the B&H cup three seasons later. They have provided a plethora of seam bowlers for England – Copson, Mike Hendrick and Alan Ward all turned out for their country and then who can forget Devon Malcolm and Dominic Cork? The limited overs team is called the Derbyshire Falcons in reference to the famous Peregrine Falcon, which nests on the city of Derby's cathedral. Previously they were known as The Scorpions and The Phantoms.

GROUNDS: The County Ground (formally known as the Racecourse) has been Derbyshire's HQ since 1871. The square at the ground was relaid in 2009/10 on a north/south axis to stop problems with the sun setting on the old east/west axis, and sun even stopped play a few years ago. Why didn't they do this sooner? Well it did set them back £100,000! In 2006 they returned to Queen's Park in Chesterfield following a multi-million pound refurbishment. The other ground used by Derbyshire is Highlands, the home of Leek and Moorlands CC, although Minor Counties side Staffordshire use the ground more frequently.

TMS ANECDOTE: Sachin Tendulkar named Queen's Park, Derbyshire's out ground, as the most beautiful ground in the world. The Little Master has obviously not been to Dagenham, complete with their high-rise tower blocks acting as natural sightscreens! Also in the 1980s the food here was the worst on the circuit, forcing away teams to call for pizzas and takeaways. One year they got a new chef in, who was superb and John Morris piled on five stone in one season! It now comes regularly second to Lord's when we ask the professionals about where the best food served on the circuit is.

BANTER FACTOR: Bowlers Tony Palladino and Jonathan Clare, and all-rounder Tim Groenewald provide the banter on Twitter. They always have something to say and the good-natured ribbing of each other keeps us Stumpers entertained!

BOOZERS: The Brunswick by the station. With a brewery on site and over 180 beers that have been brewed here, this place is legendary. Ashbourne Road is the venue for stag and hen dos that do The Mile, and this area has over twenty boozers to choose from. Days Hotel next to the ground is ok but on no account try the sausages. Mine could only have been more off-putting if I had found a blue vein running through the middle of it!

LOCAL BREW: Derby Brewing Co. produce some excellent ales including Business As Usual, a 4.4 per cent traditional amber ale that goes down easier than a drunk Abi Titmuss. If you're looking for something stronger then give Quintessential a try; it is 'complex and well-rounded with extraordinary fruit and citrus flavours', and was a winner of the Midlands Gold award in premium bitters don't ya know ... at 5.8 per cent us Stumpers will stick to a half!

OVERNIGHT STAY FACTOR: Derby as a town would get a 1/10, possibly even a nought, but I will go for a three, as some of the most beautiful scenery to be found in Britain is just a short trip away in the Peak District. Bakewell, home of the famous tart, is here, as is Chatsworth House and the Blue John caves are worth a visit. Derby itself, though, is no Paris, and is famed more for industrial production of cars and trains than for natural beauty.

CELEB WATCH: Did you know Lewis Hamilton is from Derby? Well he is ... Lewes defender Hamilton spent his younger days at Derby County before moving to London and playing for QPR and then into non-league. What do you mean not *that* Lewis Hamilton? Ellen MacArthur can be seen around Derby too, having grown up in nearby Matlock. James Morrison, no not the West Brom player but the musician (jeez I'm really confused now), is from here, while Florence Nightingale would have given people a bed bath in these parts. Henry Rolls and Charles Royce moved their factory here, while the Rolls Royce of football managers, a certain Brian Clough, lived in nearby Quarndon.

DURHAM

Durham County Cricket Club
Emirates Durham International Cricket Ground
Riverside
Chester-le-Street
County Durham
DH3 3QR

Club Colours: Blue and Yellow

The new boys of first-class cricket, having been granted this status in 1992, Durham were the Man Utd of Minor Counties cricket, winning a record-equalling 9 trophies and were the first minor county to defeat a first-class county – beating Yorkshire in the Gillette Cup in 1973. When first-class cricket came so did the names: Ian Botham, Dean Jones and Simon Hughes to name but three. The club has since become better and better with exciting young players such as all-rounder Ben Stokes knocking on the England door. Durham have provided a lot for England in the not so distant past. Paul Collingwood and Steve Harmison were members of the squad that got the Ashes in 2005, although Harmison's contribution was far greater than Colly's! Graeme Onions and Phil Mustard are the others with international experience (caught Mustard bowled Onions is still my favourite combination!). In 2008 the club won their first ever County Championship title and they retained it the year after. They have certainly come a long way in the past quarter of a century!

GROUNDS: The old Racecourse Ground is a stunning venue and was their initial home, although now home to the university cricket team. The Riverside ground, located 12 miles away from Durham in Chester-le-Street has been the home since 1995. One condition of being granted first-class status was that they build a Test match standard ground. Indeed it made the grade, hosting four England Test matches; Zimbabwe in 2003 was the first, followed by Bangladesh in 2005 and then West Indies twice two and four years later. In 2010 the club signed a groundbreaking sponsorship agreement with Emirates Airlines, with the company committing to be the main club sponsor, including stadium naming rights, for six years. It was renamed Emirates Durham

International Cricket Ground (Emirates Durham ICG or Emirates Durham). A new stand running around the ground brings the attendance up to just shy of a healthy 20,000 and it will host one of the Test matches with Australia in 2013. A hotel is due to be built by this time, along with a sparkling new entrance and a road around the ground. With the River Wear running nearby and Lumley Castle overlooking it, this is a fine place to play cricket.

TMS ANECDOTES: During the 2005 Ashes, Durham batsman Gary Pratt was brought on to field as a substitute. Pratt was fielding at cover when Damien Martyn prodded one towards him and attempted a quick single. Pratt duly threw down the stumps at the striker's end with Australian captain Ricky Ponting considerably short of his ground. Ponting, none too pleased, stormed up the steps to the dressing room and unleashed a volley of abuse at England coach Duncan Fletcher, which culminated in the whinging Aussie screaming 'You fucking cheat, Fletcher!' Ponting was angry at England's use of specialist sub-fielders while the bowlers had a rest and a shower to freshen up. That was not the case with Pratt as he was on as a sub for Simon Jones who had been taken to hospital with a serious ankle injury although this did not stop Pratt becoming the hero on the England tour bus! Also, by the River Wear in Durham is an area called The Sands. This is where the world record for throwing a cricket ball was set, and since then there have been overthrows a plenty in this part of the world.

BANTER FACTOR: Phil Mustard. Graeme Onions recently described Mustard as the funniest member of the Durham side, although he added, 'He's not actually funny, it's just that everybody laughs at him.' Nicknamed the Colonel, he must have taken a fair amount of stick!

BOOZERS: We'd recommend the Black Horse in Chester-le-Street, but the Lambton Arms with knucklehead bouncers isn't really our cup of tea. Chesters Wine Bar comes recommended by our spies, while the Queen's Head and the Butcher's Arms are the ones recommended for real ale aficionados. Durham nearby has boozers a plenty and, if there during term time, often will have some rather attractive young ladies in them. The Dun Cow is the place for good ales, while The Warehouse overlooking the river and The Boathouse are pleasant places. The Shakespeare caters for the traditionalists among us, the Market Tavern comes recommended, as does the Victoria, a listed pub. The Varsity has a nice sun terrace by the Wear, but really Durham is a pisshead's paradise with plenty to choose from.

LOCAL BREW: The Durham Brewery, based in Bowburn, use traditional English techniques to make pure, full-flavoured, natural beers. You could try the best-selling Magus at 3.8 per cent or you could be tempted in to trying Temptation at a whopping piss your pants 10 per cent! No wonder Sir Ian Botham opted to finish his career in these parts. In case you were wondering, all of their bottles are suitable for vegans!

OVERNIGHT STAY FACTOR: 9/10. Durham is quite simply a stunning place to visit. With the cathedral, the castle, the little cobbled streets and the River Wear flowing through it, we'd recommend it highly. A university city, it is the crème de la crème of the country that go here, often those who narrowly miss out on Oxford or Cambridge. Like the university, many of Durham's buildings are over 600 years old and the architecture here is amazing. The Vale of Durham nearby also offers magnificent scenery, and the coastline nearby has some great beaches. Just a short trip away is Newcastle and all that has to offer, but nearby Sunderland and Middlesbrough are not on our list of recommended places to visit. Durham, however, with the hilly meandering streets, quaint shops and river is highly recommended.

CELEBRITY WATCH: Ex-prime minister Tony Blair can often be spotted playing Scrabble in Durham, where it will be the only time he will find WMD in a rack. Rowan Atkinson originates from the city, as does fashion guru Bruce Oldfield, and Paul Collingwood is another. Record producer Trevor Horn hails from these parts, while Paddy McAloon from 1980s band Prefab Sprout was born nearby. A celebrity dwarf back in the early 1800s, Joseph Boruwlaski lived here, and, talking of small people, rugby player Andy Gomarsall is another from Durham. The man who they called a tampax (as he was in for one week and out for three), injury-prone footballer Bryan Robson can be spotted around Chester-le-Street. Finally, ex-England legends Graeme Fowler and Sir Ian Botham can often be seen strolling around this picturesque city.

ESSEX

The Ford County Ground
New Writtle Street
Chelmsford
Essex
CM2 0PG

Club Colours: Red and White

Essex have won the County Championship on six occasions, the last, however, coming twenty years ago. Some success has come in recent times, such as one-day titles in 2005 and 2006 and cup success in 2008. The men from Chelmsford were at their best in the 1980s and early 1990s, all six of their championship titles coming between 1979 and 1992. There is no coincidence that Essex's success in this period came at a time when Graham Gooch was at his peak; he scored over 30,000 runs for the club. The bowling in the first half of this period was borne by tireless left-arm seamer John Lever and spinner and prankster Ray East. As Lever passed his peak, England all-rounder Derek Pringle and fast bowler Neil Foster took over, and John Childs joined from Gloucestershire to take over as the chief spinner. The 1990s brought England internationals too. Nasser Hussain went on to captain his country in 45 Test matches and Peter Such and Mark Illott were others to pick up caps, as did current skipper James Foster. Today the future looks bright; ex-London Schools man Billy Godleman has undoubted talent, although he needs to prove how good an opener he can be. Tymal Mills is a young left-armer who will play for England, as is fellow left-arm seamer Reece Topley. In a side which includes England stars Alistair Cook and Ravi Bopara, and the likes of Owais Shah and Ryan ten Doeschate, the club is looking very healthy indeed.

GROUNDS: HQ is the County Ground, Chelmsford, a small venue which suits big hitting batsmen and high-scoring games. Graeme Napier's record 152 off 58 balls came at the ground and bowlers must hate running in from either the River End or The Hayes Close End! The large amount of passionate support Essex receives at this ground has led to it being popularly referred to as 'Fortress Chelmsford'. The other ground

being used is Castle Park in Colchester, the home of Colchester and East Essex CC. During a County Championship match at Colchester between Essex and Kent at the ground in 1938, Arthur Fagg became the only batsman ever to hit a double century in each innings. He got 244 in his first and 202 in his second.

TMS ANECDOTES: In a bad-tempered game at Southgate (the home of The Middle Stump) in 2001, Essex batsmen Ronnie Irani and Darren Robinson were batting on a main road. Phil Tufnell, the celebrity jungle man and one-time England and Middlesex left-arm spinner, was having a torrid time of it. Nearer the end of his career, Tufnell just didn't have the love of the game that he once had and let the jovial Irani wind him up to the point where Robinson tucked one into the leg side for a single and Tufnell was not amused. Tuffers then proceeded to exchange some harsh words with Robinson and kicked him flat out in the shin! Graeme Gooch, coach of Essex at the time, had the raging Ivana (the pair had umpteen barneys when Gooch was the England ruler – sorry, captain) and Tufnell knew it was time to hang 'em up!

Mark Ilott is a funny man as well. Once in the showers at Chelmsford after a game versus the touring West Indians, Mark found himself in between the rather well-endowed Ottis Gibson and Junior Murray. Brian Lara came in and informed the left-armer that he didn't own a cock, he in fact owned a clitoris!

BANTER FACTOR: Many a former Essex man has had something to say. From Ray East to Ronnie Irani and Darren Gough, they have always loved a giggle. Nowadays young Tymal Mills doesn't mind exchanging some banter via Twitter! The man every girl wants, however, is bus driver Marc Marangou!

BOOZERS: The Orange Tree in Lower Anchor Street comes highly recommended and is a haunt of the Essex team as well. The Plough in Duke Street is also recommended, but unfortunately you will find the famous Dukes nightclub sadly no longer. This was the venue where Mervyn Westfield and Danish Kaneria did their dirty work in the match-fixing scandal. My advice is to leave the city of Chelmsford behind, and go to the quaint village of Stock nearby. Head for the Hoop, a great little venue that has its own festival, normally in early June.

LOCAL BREW: The BBC rule the roost round here – that is the Brentwood Beer Company by the way. Best at 4.2 or Gold at 4.3 per cent is recommended, but if you really fancy getting pissed quickly then choose Chockwork Orange at nearly 6 per cent, Essex Man's tipple!

OVERNIGHT STAY FACTOR: 5/10. Chelmsford itself is just another commuter town based in the south-east taking people into Liverpool Street to work in the City of London. A couple of riverside developments are quite pleasant but it is nothing spectacular, without actually being ugly. Marconi based his factory here, which the Luftwaffe targeted so, therefore, a lot of the history has disappeared. Still, it was voted the eighth nicest place to live in the UK – the schools are good and crime is relatively low. It just doesn't have that wow factor of other places on the circuit.

CELEBRITY WATCH: If you are lucky you might miss the 'stars' of *The Only Way is Essex*, although a man who looks like he should be in the show, Jeff Brazier, lives in the area. Joe Thomas from the *Inbetweeners* is also seen around, although he is reported to be much better behaved in real life. Former Villa goalkeeper and European Cup winner Nigel Spink can also be seen hanging around between the sticks of local parks, while you could also be Searching (Looking for Love) with 1980s singer Hazell Dean. I know what you're thinking, you're going to dust off that autograph book right away, aren't you?

GLAMORGAN

Glamorgan
Glamorgan County Cricket Club
SWALEC Stadium
Cardiff
CF11 9XR

Club Colours: Dark Blue and Red (like the local football team, can be subject to change!)

Since 1921 the club have been Wales' sole representative in the English County Championship – a competition they won in 1948, 1969 and 1997. Glamorgan have also beaten all of the major Test-playing nations, including Australia, who they defeated in successive tours in 1964 and 1968. Glamorgan have also been successful in the one-day game. They won the National League in 1993 and 2002, as well as reaching the Lord's final of the Gillette Cup in 1977 and the Benson & Hedges competition in 2000. Don Sheppard was the greatest player to never play for England. One of the great county bowlers, he took more first-class wickets, 2,218 at 21.32 each. Players who did play for England, however, include father and son duo Jeff and Simon Jones, Steve 'Sid' James, Robert Croft and Matthew Maynard. If you add the overseas superstars that have graced Sophia Gardens – Viv Richards, Waqar Younis, Ravi Shastri and Sourav Ganguly to name a few – you can see how attractive Glamorgan have become. Nowadays, under the tutelage of Mark Wallace, there are lots of young exciting players down in Cardiff. James Harris is a future England star and Huw Waters looks like he has many good years ahead of him. With the never aging Croft and Dean Cosker still tweaking it and the good solid overseas signings that keep coming, it won't be long until Glam are back in the top division fighting for the title.

GROUNDS: SWALEC in Cardiff, St Helen's in Swansea, Abergavenny, Colwyn Bay.

TMS ANECDOTEs: Glamorgan legend Greg Thomas was once bowling at Sir Vivian Richards in a game at Cardiff between Glamorgan and Somerset. After beating the legendary Antiguan outside the off stump Thomas gave him a bit of gyp by saying, 'It's red, it is round and weighs four and a half ounces, can't you see it?' Next ball Thomas bangs one in, and Vivi deposits him into the River Taff. He walks down the wicket to the crestfallen Welshman and says, 'You know what it looks like, now go and fetch it!'

BANTER FACTOR: The Glamorgan boys are full of banter, but Gareth Rees and skipper Mark Wallace have the best. If they are not slagging off James Harris' Friday night disco pants then they are on Steve 'Sid' James' case, calling him a nerd. They also like to wind up Robert Croft for being a geriatric although, in fairness, he gives as good as he gets!

BOOZERS: There are plenty to choose from along St Mary Street and one of the finest is the Cottage. It's an old pub – long and narrow – but full of characters. It's never quiet and that seems to be a good sign. The Owain Glyndwr is also well worth an outing. It's a big rugby pub with excellent beer and lively banter – just stay away if there is a rugby international on. Even more so if you're English! Closer to the ground practice your Cymraeg in the Mochyn Du (The Black Pig), the Cayo or the Cricketers. Often you will find the Glammy boys having an après match pint.

LOCAL BREW: Look no further than S.A. Brains. The company owns over 250 pubs across South Wales. The Brains Best is particularly well looked after in this area and even Bumble refers to it as 'a great drop that gets my vote more often than not.' There is stronger Brains stuff too and there are also seasonal varieties. St David's Ale is brewed to celebrate St David's Day and is available in February and March, while Taff End is available in June and July and celebrates sponsorship of the Glamorgan. Brains' link with Glamorgan Cricket dates back to 1891, when Joseph H. Brain took over the captaincy of the Glamorgan cricket team. Joseph is credited as a leading light in the club's early development when games were played in the field behind the old Cardiff Arms Hotel – the field that has since become famous all over the world as Cardiff Arms Park. Two years later, William H. Brain achieved a wicket-keeping feat that has still never been equalled – three stumpings off consecutive balls in a first-class fixture. Brains has been a sponsor of Glamorgan Cricket since 2001, including shirt sponsorship for several years. They now provide the Official Beer of Glamorgan Cricket, which is available throughout the SWALEC. The other brew our spies recommend is the Artisan Brewing Company in Pontcanna.

OVERNIGHT STAY FACTOR: 8/10. If you like a castle or three, then Cardiff is the place to visit. With one in the heart of the city, the fairy tale Castell Coch in nearby Radyr (the cause of many a crash on the M4, which it overlooks) and Caerphilly just up the road, then you are spoilt for choice. The Bay was transformed a few years ago from a red light district into one of the smartest parts of the UK, and there are a plethora of attractions around here. St Fagans Welsh Museum is nearby, and Cardiff generally is great for shopping and for nightlife. Llandaff with its stunning cathedral is worth a snoop around too. A bit further afield, Dan yr Ogof caves will keep the kids happy, and Big Pit, a disused mine near Cwmbran is educational and interesting, with tours run by ex-miners. For those slightly older, Caroline Street, or Chip Alley as it is known, is a great place to people watch, especially at 2 a.m.! One thing you won't be short of in this part of the world is a warm welcome from the locals. Top people.

CELEBRITY WATCH: Matthew Pritchard of *Dirty Sanchez* fame can often be seen putting a stapler through his balls for a laugh in one of Cardiff's many watering holes, while Charlotte Church is often seen parading her latest boyfriend around the docks. Musically Cardiff has provided us with lots over the years, from Shirley Bassey and Shakin' Stevens

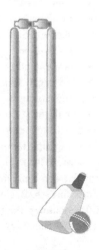

to Cerys Matthews of Catatonia, Noel Gallagher's mate Andy Bell from Oasis and High Flying Birds, and The Automatic. If a local comes up to you and says he is a member of the Soul Crew, then this is nothing to do with the local music and we would recommend you vacate the local vicinity quickly! Rob Brydon and Griff Rhys Jones provide the comedy, while you may see James Harries mincing around the Bay – not the Glamorgan bowler, but *That's Life* antique expert, child prodigy and David Gower lookalike transsexual, who now goes by the name of Lauren, after swapping his bat and balls for a crease! Newsreader John Humphrys and Wales rugby captain Sam Warburton like a Brains or two, while from the world of football, Craig Bellamy will show you his golf swing and Ryan Giggs will show you his brotherly love.

GLOUCESTERSHIRE

Nevil Road
The County Ground
Bristol
BS7 9EJ

Club Colours: Fawn, Brown, Pale Grey, Dark Green, Red and Navy Blue!

Gloucestershire were *the* side to support in the 1890s and the Grace brothers (no not from 1970s comedy *Are You Being Served?*, but E.M. and the more famous W.G.) were bringing huge crowds into Bristol. Four championships arrived during this period, and even in the early twentieth century, the 'Croucher' Gilbert Jessop scored runs for fun. Many lean years followed, although the 1970s brought one-day success thanks to the exploits of the brilliant Mike Proctor, and who can forget that famous one-day hat-trick televised back then? Proctor wasn't the only overseas to do well though, as Sadiq Mohammed and, more prominently, Zaheer Abbas made hay on the West Country tracks. In the 1980s famous players such as the West Indian Courtney Walsh and our own Jack Russell were the main men, but it was the early millennium under Mark 'Boo-Boo' Alleyne and coach John Bracewell which brought a host of one-day glory. Now the likes of Dan Housego, the talented Benny Howell, David Payne, Ian Saxelby and Chris Dent have plenty to live up to as this once proud club struggles to retain their former glories.

GROUNDS: Bristol and Cheltenham. The festival at the glorious Cheltenham College is the oldest to be played on an out ground, the school having hosted matches since 1872. Bristol is a ground which doesn't do a beautiful city justice if we're honest. Based a couple of miles north of the centre up the A38, otherwise known as the Gloucester Road, the ground is hemmed between houses and isn't the easiest to find! The ends are the Nevil Road End, or the Ashley Down End, not to be confused with Downend further up the M32, and birthplace of the doctor! It has an old pavilion which is set back slightly from the pitch and the Jessop Stand which has a peculiar roof, but has character, and the rest of the ground is empty space. Temporary seating is brought in for big games, and Bristol hosted its first international in 1999. Plans are in place to regenerate the venue including a conference facility and plans for 147 flats, which should bring this ground into the twenty-first century. Nearby, over the other side of the Gloucester Road, was where the *Young Ones* was filmed, and the bank they famously robbed was the swimming baths. In the other direction is Brunel Technical College which doubled up as the set for *Casualty*. See, this book can be educational as well as just purely smutty!

TMS ANECDOTES: W.G. Grace was renowned as a great player but he was also a cheating bastard, putting it bluntly. After being bowled first ball in a well-attended charity game, he merely put the bails back on and said, 'They came to see me bat and not you bowl.' If talking to the locals here, do not be worried if they put an L on the end of words that end in a vowel. Bristolians will regularly talk about having 'good ideals' and 'shopping trips to Asdal'. Rumour has it, the city used to be called Bristow, before the locals decided to chuck an l on the end!

BANTER FACTOR: John Bracewell. The Kiwi coach regularly takes the piss out of his players, according to Benny Howell. A number of the Gloucestershire players are fans of The Middle Stump, and they rate the banter.

BOOZERS: Around the ground you have plenty on the Gloucester Road. Robin Hood's Retreat comes recommended by my spies, while the Sportsman with its thirteen pool tables and big screens everywhere is a mecca of testosterone! Further afield head to the Cadbury House in bohemian Montpelier, a great venue, although now bereft of the famous Wurlitzer jukebox. Get a cab to Clifton and Racks wine bar in St Paul's Road is the favourite of the Glos players, while the White Lion Bar and the stunning terrace is not a place to fuck about on, with a drop over the gorge of 600ft, and the amazing Clifton Suspension Bridge up to your right. What a view, although those with vertigo will get brown trousers! In the centre there are thousands of bars, although for atmosphere try the cobbled King Street, and the Llandoger Trow.

LOCAL BREW: Bristol Bass is a local beer very popular, although at the time of going to press we are not sure if you can still get Smiles, which was an old brewery in Cotham. Cotham was a place where The Middle Stump's Dan was ejected from a Tandoori once for throwing a lemon into a revolving fan and it hitting a bloke in the other corner! I digress. Butcombe Bitter, just the other way down the A38, is a lovely pint and we would recommend it highly at 4.2 per cent. Perfect.

OVERNIGHT STAY FACTOR: 9/10. I love Bristol, but then I lived there as a student. So much to do in the centre, such as Brunel's Suspension Bridge or go and have a look around the boat, the SS *Great Britain*. @Bristol is their science museum-type place, while the zoo there is one of the best in the country. Meander around the docks

(where we once raved in warehouse parties in the late 1980s before it was all redeveloped), browse the shops on Park Street (where at the bottom you have the cathedral and College Green), or venture further afield to Weston-super-Mare or Cheddar. If staying in Bristol, then Clifton Village is well worth pottering around. So much to do, you could almost even stay for two nights.

CELEBRITY WATCH: Good music has come out of Bristol in the past including Massive Attack, Portishead and the Brilliant Corners. While here you could meet local artist Banksy if anyone knew who he was, while bearded Bristolian Justin Lee Collins can also be spotted, offering more control of his girlfriend than your average Mike Proctor over. Porn stars Cathy Barry and Michelle Thorne can show you their Avon Gorge, while Cary Grant was born here. Writers Dick King-Smith and Tom Stoppard were from these parts, as is comedian, sorry football manager Ian Holloway. Finally, another man who hails from this city is someone who went to Buckingham Palace in 2003 after England won the Rugby World Cup. As the players were sitting there trying to be polite, one of the royal equerries come over all suited and booted and offered him a cup of tea.

'Lovely, yes please Babb,' he replied in his West Country accent to which the butler replied, 'Earl Grey?' The rugby player shot out his hand and said, 'Pleased to meet you Earl, I'm Mark Regan!'

HAMPSHIRE

The Ageas Bowl
Botley Road
West End
Southampton
SO30 3XH

Club Colours: Blue and Gold

Cricket was rumoured to have originated in Hampshire with Hambledon CC being founded on Broadpenny Down and cricket was even supposed to have been played at Winchester College beforehand. However, they were an unfashionable county and even lost their first-class status for a while before regaining it. Under the wonderful Colin Ingleby-MacKenzie in 1961 they gained their first County Championship, and another arrived in 1973, thanks to an outstanding opening pair of Gordon Greenidge and Barry Richards. Malcolm Marshall was another who lit up Southampton in the 1980s, along with Robin Smith who played here for twenty-three years. A move to the Rose Bowl occurred in 2001, leaving the atmospheric but hemmed-in Northlands Road, and the arrival of Shane Warne and Dominic Cork brought more success, along with the cult hero of the south coast, Dimi Mascarenhas. Now in financial difficulty – so much so that they had to sell the Bowl back to the local council – they still have an excellent youth policy meaning the likes of Danny Briggs, Chris Wood, Sean Terry and Michael Bates keep the traditions of this fine cricketing county alive. James Vince, Liam Dawson and David Balcombe, meanwhile, all have England aspirations.

GROUNDS: Southampton; May's Bounty, Basingstoke; United Services at Portsmouth and Dean Park in Bournemouth. The Bowl, whether it is Ageas or of the Rose variety, while a fine venue, is an out-of-town ground, smart and shiny but lacking the character of the old Northlands Road. Traffic can also be a pain in the arse here as well, especially for big events such as a Test match or the T20 finals. You enter by the second XI ground, and the main pavilion is the showpiece of the ground.

There is a bit of double-tiered action to the left and right of this poor man's Mound Stand but the rest is a bowl .... strange, that. For internationals the ground has extra seating which miraculously appears, which makes most of the stands two tiered, so check the website beforehand. Having gone over budget, the ground nearly put Hampshire out of business, and only time will tell whether the building of a 25,000-seater out-of-town stadium was the right thing to do.

TMS ANECDOTES: Colin Ingleby-McKenzie was a fine man and the captain of the Hants side who won the championship in 1961. Having made some outrageously brave declarations, he was asked what was behind his team winning. His reply that he 'insisted his team were in bed before breakfast', is a man that makes him a legend in the eyes of the boys at The Middle Stump.

BANTER FACTOR: Dimi Mascarenhas or Chris Wood, who has been known to run around the Rose Bowl in his pants, now Shane Warne has left. The Australian leggie gets respect for having a threesome with a couple of young ladies a few years back in a Kensington hotel, before driving back to Southampton in the early hours to take seven wickets to lead his side to victory. Shaun Udal was another who had decent banter, along with the Judge, Robin Smith. Hampshire, since the days of John Arlott's burr, has always been a factory of rhetoric.

BOOZERS: Being an out-of-town stadium there are plenty of bars in the ground. However, the White Swan in Mansbridge Road is quite decent and offers a decent carvery too. Around West End is the Master Builder which offers some decent ale, while the Two Brothers offer a warm welcome (a place for Ryan Giggs to visit?). Closer to the ground the Southampton Arms is decent in an olde worlde type way, and the West End Brewery closest to the Bowl is fairly grotty.

LOCAL BREW: Loads of microbreweries are springing up in the south, but the Ringwood Brewery based in the heart of the New Forest produces the water that the locals drink. Their Best Ale at 3.8 per cent is the most popular but the 49er at 4.9 per cent and the Old Thumper, named after Nigel Cowley, at 5.6 per cent must mean that the residents of Hampshire are consistently pissed.

OVERNIGHT STAY FACTOR: 7/10. Southampton itself is no oil painting. An industrial port, still a working dock which is based in the heart of the city, the Germans ruined it during the war, and as such, much of the architecture is 1950s. Close by, however, the New Forest with villages such as Lymington and the wild ponies frolicking throughout the countryside round this up to a respectable seven. Bournemouth is worth a visit if only for the golden sands, while there are some stunning venues over the water on the Isle of Wight. Pompey is twenty miles away with the *Mary Rose* and HMS *Victory*. The two port cities of Southampton and Portsmouth seriously despise each other. Very much Royal Navy v Merchant Navy, a strike in the 1930s where Sotonians went back to work have always made them labelled Scummers by their Portsmouth counterparts, and the two football teams don't like each other much either.

CELEBRITY WATCH: The wonderful punk/folk singer Frank Turner can be seen in nearby Winchester, while the not so wonderful Craig David also hails from these parts. Mr Smooth, Colin Firth keeps the ladies of Southampton from their docks drying out, as well as another old smoothie Lord David Gower, who surveys his manor in nearby Chilworth, often ordering the serfs and peasants around. The king who has terrified dyslexics for years, Cnut (have I got that right?) was crowned here, while Benny Hill would also chase the ladies in this part of Hampshire. The Black Prince, Edward hailed from here and Jane Austen showed her *Sense and Sensibility* in this port, while Captain Smith, who hit an iceberg in a boat called the *Titanic*, didn't! Talking of leaking, glamour model Lucy Pinder is another resident, while Olympic hero Ben Ainslie is from nearby Lymington. Scott Mills completes the list in this autograph hunter's paradise.

KENT

The St Lawrence Ground
Old Dover Road
Canterbury
Kent
CT1 3NZ

Club Colours: Maroon and Blue

Kent is a county full of history and one that has achieved much over the years. The era before the First World War was a halcyon period for the county known as the 'garden of England', while the 1930s with Leslie Ames and Frank Woolley were also outstanding. Woolley scored just shy of 50,000 runs and retired at nearly fifty years of age. The 1970s were a great period and the elderly Colin Cowdrey, along with Alan Ealham, John Shepherd, Asif Iqbal, 'Deadly' Derek Underwood and others brought success to the St Lawrence Ground. Now the likes of Sam Billings and the highly rated Daniel Bell-Drummond are hoping to bring Division One cricket back here after being relegated from the top tier for the first time ever in their long and illustrious history. The supporters of this county are some of the most passionate and knowledgeable on the circuit and one thing they recognise is a good wicketkeeper. Leslie Ames, Godfrey Evans, Alan Knott, Paul Downton and Geraint Jones have all represented both Kent and England.

GROUNDS: The St Lawrence Ground, Canterbury; Beckenham; Maidstone and the Nevill Ground, Tunbridge Wells. The ground at Tunbridge Wells is a quaint enclosure, while playing at the old Lloyds Bank ground in Beckenham is an attempt to tap into the crowded commuter belt of south-east London, although this venue is a mere five miles from The Oval, yet over sixty from Canterbury!

The St Lawrence has been redeveloped a lot in recent years, and you can enter via the Old Dover Road or the Nackington Road. A collection of small stands all in differing styles greet you on one side of the ground, all named after famous Kent legends. All around the stadium are small food venues and Jonesey's in the Les Ames Pavilion is worth a visit. The famous lime tree is now back within the playing arena after the the original 200-year-old one was lost in the wind. This is one of two first-class grounds in the world to have a tree, the other being in Pietermaritzburg. A health and fitness club, conference suites and new hospitality areas complete the venue. Canterbury Week is a

fine festival with prizes awarded for things like the best ladies' hat, and is normally very well attended. As mentioned this can be one of the more raucous venues on the circuit, and they can get quite partisan at times, especially after a day on the Spitfire. Enjoy Canterbury, it's an honest and traditional ground, full of character. You know, the sort of place where the crowd have a knockabout on the outfield during the tea interval.

TMS ANECDOTES: Down at Canterbury they seem not to be too fond of their rivals over at Sussex. One wag told me a story one day that went something like this, 'Following a tough season James Kirtley booked a relaxing sea cruise for two, having established that Rob Key was neither a passenger nor crewmember. Enjoying a stroll on deck with his mother one evening, James was concerned to see an elderly lady standing next to the rail and shouting hysterically, "Help, help, my husband's fallen overboard, someone throw him a lifebelt." James rushed to the nearest lifebelt, picked it up, rubbed it vigorously on his trousers, paced out 18 yards, turned and ran in ...'

Another was Bob Monkhouse, who was a Kent cricket fan born in Beckenham, and used to say that people shouted the county of his birth after him wherever he went! Lastly, the gentlemen supporting Kent will either be Men of Kent, or Kentish Men. It all depends on which side of the River Medway you were born in, with Canterbury being Men of Kent, while those towards the west of the county being Kentish Men.

BANTER FACTOR : Rob Key. The Kent captain has to tone it down a bit more these days with the responsibility of captaincy, but he was the man who had people chuckling back in the late 1990s. A big mate of Flintoff and Harmison, he has kept cricketers on the circuit entertained with his one-liners for years.

BOOZERS: Directly outside the ground is the Bat and Ball but it is often packed, and not that great on the occasion I last visited a few years back. It may have changed and let's hope the hair served with my lunch that day is no longer on the menu. Head into the city centre, to places such as the City Arms in Butchery Lane (a fifteenth-century inn and a real ale lover's paradise), and a host of other pubs, often packed with nubile student, touristy types and serving a far better pint. The Foundry in White Horse Lane is a great place with the Canterbury Brewers

microbrewery on site, and you can see the ales being made within the city walls. Canterbury has some fantastic venues, but be careful though, as it is a squaddie place and we don't want any of our readers to end up feeling like they have had a shoeing off Invicta, the famous Kent horse.

LOCAL BREW: Try the beers from the Canterbury Brewers at the above mentioned Foundry, which is well worth a visit. Shepherd Neame are Britain's oldest brewer and their range of ales are the stuff to drink in the garden of England. By the way, if it is the garden, then do not go to Gillingham, the compost heap! Canterbury Jack ale is named after roguish fairground characters from yesteryear, who got up to some dodgy antics. Anyone who has had a one-night stand won't like the sound of their Late Red at 4.5 per cent, but Whitstable Bay with a few oysters goes down a treat. Spitfire at 4.2 per cent, and that favourite of the choristers of Canterbury Cathedral, Bishop's Finger, is extremely popular.

OVERNIGHT STAY FACTOR: 9/10. One of the most famous tourist hotspots of the UK, Canterbury, with the cathedral looming large over the city, is great to stay in. Walk down little cobbled streets, cross beautiful bridges spanning the river or just have a browse through the many shops that this town houses. Now just a fifty-five-minute trip from London by train thanks to the Channel Tunnel route, the area around offers great scenery too. Whitstable is worth a visit with the famous oysters, while John Aspinall's zoos – Howletts and Port Lympne – are famous for the tigers snacking on the odd keeper. For those of the bucket and spade brigade, have a 'Jolly Boys' Outing' to Margate or those of a patriotic nature can go and visit the nearby White Cliffs of Dover.

There is lots of history here too, with the Battle of Britain and the heroic locals who sailed to Dunkirk.

CELEBRITY WATCH: David Gower went to school here you know, while TV presenter Fiona Phillips also spent her early years here. Sir Freddie Laker, whose airlines made Easyjet look luxurious, was another from the town, as is Orlando Bloom. Cultural writers Christopher Marlowe and Mary Tourtel who created Rupert the Bear are from here, while ecclesiastical bearded wonder Dr Rowan Williams can be spotted around the town. Ellie Goulding provides the music, while Alan Davies provides the erm, comedy. Finally see if you can spot the ghost of Geoffrey Chaucer, who wrote the *Canterbury Tales*, a rude, crude medieval piece of wit about a bunch of pissheads, and forerunner of *Cricket Banter* by The Middle Stump.

LANCASHIRE

Talbot Road
Old Trafford
Manchester
M16 0PX

Club Colours: Red

Lancashire are a huge county. Think football, think Manchester United and City, Liverpool and Everton all rolled into one, along with the other sides in the region and you'll see the sporting potential here. Founded in 1864, a chap called Johnny Briggs made hay in the early years here, although I don't think it was the same guy who played Mike Baldwin in *Corrie* all those years later! Archie McLaren was another big scorer, racking up a mere 422 once, but despite the likes of Cyril Washbrook, good times after 1950 were elusive, chasing the Holy Grail of the County Championship, which they didn't win until 2011. One-day success was almost a certainty and who can ever forget David Hughes smashing Proctor in the dark in 1971, as the trains rattled down the side of the ground? Clive Lloyd and Farokh Engineer added to the home-grown legends such as David Lloyd, Frank Hayes, while the later years brought England opening bats Graeme Fowler and Mike Atherton. The 1990s brought success with the likes of Andrew Flintoff, Glen Chapple and the like. However, it was the home-grown, no-frills side that won in 2011 under Chapple and the coaching of Peter Moores, ending the meagre years, thinner than a character in a painting by that Mancunian legend, L.S. Lowry. Financial pressures have hit the club hard with the redevelopment of Old Trafford and a protracted legal battle, but Lancy Lancy look like they will remain at the top of the English game for a long time to come yet.

GROUNDS: Old Trafford, Aigburth, Southport and Lytham St Annes. Aigburth in Liverpool has a charming pavilion with many steps leading to the pitch, but Old Trafford and the redevelopment is what is whetting the whistle of most Lancastrians. What you notice about the ground is not the charming pavilion, which has stood for years, with a Long Room and history a plenty. No, it is this huge red monstrosity from the outside next door to its ageing neighbour, as out of place as Vera Duckworth's stone cladding! Inside, however, it is amazing, housing over 1,000 corporate guests at a time and The Point is for twenty-first-century cricket watching. I believe it is going to get an identical brother and a sister over the other side of the ground shortly, and the comings and goings at Old Trafford when it comes to stands, which are up and down quicker than the knickers of Wayne Rooney's latest hooker, cannot be written about as they will have no doubt changed by the time this book is published. A hotel overlooks one side, and not content with changing the stands constantly, they even changed the direction of the square. Time stands still for no Mancunian.

TMS ANECDOTES: Frank Hayes. Frank Fish, as he was known, was a maverick or lunatic depending on your point of view, but was known for his ability to drink heavily in one session, then turn up and bat the next day. All these Lancastrians went big – Jack Simmons could eat four portions of fish and chips in one sitting, Ian Austin could eat two or three curries, Andrew Flintoff was no stranger to the beer jugs, and Patrick Patterson was rumoured to have had one of the biggest appendages ever in the whole game. The only thing small about Lancashire players was 5ft 3in Harry Pilling.

BANTER FACTOR: Not a current player but Lancastrian legend Graeme Fowler, who has helped me no end with this book, and has been a superstar. His Fifty Shades of Graeme on Twitter produced some quality moments and the man is one of the funniest around. If you ever meet him, feel free to ask him about the time Joel Garner smashed his box.

BOOZERS: These can get seriously busy – and I do mean busy. The Trafford and the Bishop Blaize are decent near to the ground but give Cloud 23 a go on the higher floors of the Hilton in the city centre, for a panoramic view of the city. Dukes 92 is a decent venue, as is the Banyan Tree in Castlefield, a short walk along the canal to OT. Deansgate in the centre is worth a visit, and not forgetting a good curry in Rusholme afterwards. Again, take your pick among many on the famous curry mile.

LOCAL BREW: Marble Brewery and Boddingtons were the Mancunian beers of choice but we are going to plump for the famous Thwaites of Blackburn. Bumble swears by them. Lancaster Bomber and Nutty Black are both decent, but Smooth Old Dan at 6.5 per cent, named after one of the co-writers of The Middle Stump is what Frank Hayes would drink. Loads of microbreweries are here as well, and Manchester is legendary when it comes to beer.

OVERNIGHT STAY FACTOR: 8/10. Manchester is a city with loads of history and well worth a visit. The regeneration of the city means that the Smiths' line, 'Oh Manchester, so much to answer for' is regarded no longer. There is Castlefield with the science museum, the historic buildings, a trip around the set of *Coronation Street*, a tour around the football ground of Old Trafford, or Urbis, a great museum. The cathedral and art gallery here are both worth a visit, especially for fans of Lowry or Bacon. Alternatively, go celeb spotting in one of the local suburbs such as Alderley Edge or Hale.

CELEBRITY WATCH: Some of the finest music in history has been made by both Manchester and Liverpool, but the Republic of Mancunia has given us The Smiths, The Stone Roses, New Order, The Inspiral Carpets, Happy Mondays, Oasis, Joy Division, The Buzzcocks, Joyce Sims, The Doves and loads more. Unfortunately it has also given us Gary Barlow. Bernard Manning hailed from these parts, as did Les Dawson. Judy Finnigan can be spotted around town, as can many of the *Coronation Street* stars, Man City and United players. Finally Frank Sidebottom hailed from nearby Altrincham, while the ghost of Eddie Yeats cleans the bins in nearby Salford.

LEICESTERSHIRE

The County Ground
Grace Road
Leicester
LE2 8AD

Club Colours: Green and Red

Leicestershire were a county who were also-rans until the 1970s, when the likes of Ray Illingworth and David Gower transformed them into one of the best sides in the country. The Benson & Hedges Cup was won in 1972, as was the County Championship in 1975. With Peter Willey, Jonathan Agnew, Phil De Freitas and Chris Lewis among their alumni the 1980s should have been a better period, but it was the 1990s with Paul Nixon and James Whitaker as coach that brought the halcyon years to the Midlands. Two County Championships arrived in this time, along with England honours for a number of their players, but times have been tough for the Foxes in recent years, apart from this amazing ability to win the T20. Always a county who have produced numerous home-grown players, financial troubles mean they are now at the mercy of other clubs, and the likes of James Taylor, Stuart Broad and Harry Gurney have all departed Grace Road in recent years. Let's hope they keep the likes of Wayne White, Shiv Thakor and Josh Cobb in years to come, at this proud and homely venue.

GROUNDS: Grace Road, Hinckley, Rutland School. Grace Road is one of the most maligned venues on the county circuit. The ground is a collection of low-lying stands, apart from the two ends. At the Pavilion End, the Charles Palmer Suite offers a fine carvery at the weekends, while at the Bennett End, a barbecue is often lit up behind the pavilion. This end also houses the indoor school and numerous other bars and refreshment stands adorn this ground. The Leicester crowd are always full of banter, are often good fun and can get passionate, especially during their beloved T20. One of the most multicultural areas of England produces an ethnically diverse crowd and the local Indian and West Indian communities often add value to Grace Road. Based two miles out of the city centre, this isn't a glamour ground by any account, but well worth a visit when full.

TMS ANECDOTES: When Bobby Simpson took over as Leicester coach back in the early 1990s, he would often throw a barbecue event round at his house to help foster team spirit. These were often alcohol free, but the more enterprising Leicestershire players would turn up with a bottle of vodka poured into a bottle of coke and no one would know any better. This was all going fine, until Simpson's three-year-old grandson got hold of the 'coke' and drank it liberally before falling around all over the garden.

BANTER FACTOR: Lewis Springett. The West Indian with the Hawaiian shirts was a huge Leicester fan, but is sadly no longer with us. His shout of 'Brandy Time' when a Leicester batsman hit runs was well known around Grace Road, or 'Leave the gate open' to the stewards, when an opposition batsman went out to bat. Paul Nixon was another known for his banter, and his retirement means that Leicester is a much quieter place to visit these days without these two characters of the game.

BOOZERS: The Cricketers located on Grace Road is a typical estate pub if I'm honest and can get busy during games as can that famous watering hole of the local nunnery, the Dry Dock. My advice is head for the Black Horse in Aylestone, with a friendly landlord, and guest beers aplenty.

Further towards the city centre, try a place called The Pub. With fifteen hand-pulled real ales, this is a boozer sent down from God himself and a place worth half an hour of anyone's time.

LOCAL BREW: Everards is the beer of choice for the East Midlanders, and their Tiger Ale, not to be confused with Tiger Beer is very popular. Original at 5.2 per cent is a top beer, and those who like a lager should try the Sunchaser, which is best served chilled. Also, the Rutland Brewery with beers brewed in the UK's smallest county are well worth a try.

OVERNIGHT STAY FACTOR: 1/10. Leicester is not a pretty place, but the one thing it has got in its favour is the multiculturalism which means a variety of different cuisines on offer. Some great curry houses await if you find yourself here, but seriously I wouldn't bother taking your missus away for a weekend to Leicester, unless you wish to break up with her.

CELEBRITY WATCH: David Icke is a resident of Leicester and will happily spread his brand of paranoia around, while Kasabian are a better endorsement of the city. Jug-eared crisp eater Gary Lineker hails from here, as do Martin Johnson, Emile Heskey and Dion Dublin. John Emburey fan, Tony Allcock the ex-bowls player is another, while Peter Shilton can often be spotted having a flutter on the cricket with one of Leicester's Indian bookmakers. Dickie Attenborough will call you a 'luvvie darling' if he sees you, while David will quietly observe the town species fighting on a Friday night, in the name of Natural History. Finally, Gok Wan's parents own a Chinese restaurant just outside the city, where you could always have a 69 with him. That's the Beef in Black Bean sauce, as opposed to seeing Gok look good naked!

MIDDLESEX

Middlesex County Cricket Club
Lord's Cricket Ground
St John's Wood
London
NW8 8QN

Club Colours: Navy Blue and White

With fourteen County Championship titles behind them including Second Division and shared, Middlesex are one of the most decorated sides in England. The county of Middlesex now only appears as a postal district to the north-east, north-west and west of London, but the county represents all those who live north of the River Thames. With another eight trophies in the one-day game to their name, they went through a drought until a record-breaking score in the T20 at the Rose Bowl in 2008 saw them lift their first piece of silverware in fifteen years. A name change swiftly followed as the Crusaders was deemed offensive to the local Jewish and Muslim communities around NW8, and they are now known as the Middlesex Panthers. With a hall of fame including some of the greats of English cricket such as Bill Edrich, Denis Compton, Jack Robertson, Mike Brearley, Mike Gatting, Phil Edmonds, John Emburey, Phil Tufnell and Andrew Strauss you can smell the history and the nostalgia with this club. Some fine youngsters are coming through and it remains to be seen whether the likes of Joe Denly, Sam Robson, Toby Roland-Jones and Ollie Wilkin can live up to their predecessors on the hallowed turf.

GROUNDS: Lord's, Richmond, Southgate and Uxbridge. Where do we start with Lord's? The home of cricket is one of the best days out in London, and you can even see the view to the wicket as you urinate in the member's toilets in the pavilion! Start by turning left out of St John's Wood tube and follow the crowd. The first gate you come to on Wellington Road offers you a chance to look at the practice nets, and the Nursery ground. Ignore this and further on you have the famous Grace Gates on St John's Wood Road, which leads you around the back of the main pavilion, home to the famous Long Room and honours boards on the dressing room. Straight opposite you from here is the media centre hovering over the Nursery End, still looking like Cherie Blair's mouth. To the left you have the Grandstand, but to the right is where The Middle Stump boys prefer to be ... like a Friday night, snuggled in the Mound! To the left of this is the Tavern, where the more boisterous tend to gather. Look out for the weather vane, Old Father Time, in the South East corner of the ground. The MCC Museum is also worth a day trip alone.

TMS ANECDOTES: Mike Gatting, a fan of the finest food in the country at Lord's, was once fielding at slip and his skipper David Gower once asked the bowler, Chris Cowdrey, 'Would you like Gatt a little wider?' The response was, 'If Gatt gets any wider, he'll burst.'

BANTER FACTOR: Tim Murtagh is known to drop in the odd short one and follow it up with words, and Gareth Berg is a character. Ex-overseas player Justin Langer was never short of a word or two either.

BOOZERS: The Tavern is on site and you can even sample real ales made at Lord's. On Test match days head towards Kilburn, and the Clifton Hotel is a good venue, with character and atmosphere. Plenty of guest ales here!

LOCAL BREW: Fuller's is the Middlesex brewery and still have their brewery in Chiswick, with what is reputed to be the oldest wisteria in Britain growing around it. London Pride is their main seller, along with Chiswick beer, while the ESB at 5.9 per cent will certainly put hairs on your chest!

OVERNIGHT STAY FACTOR: 10/10. 'When a man is tired of London, he is tired of life,' said Samuel Johnson and Lord's is right on the doorstep of the West End, or close to Hampstead. Plenty of nightlife abounds, as do tourist venues, although bring a few shekels with you as it isn't a cheap city. Big Ben, the Houses of Parliament, Westminster Abbey, Oxford Street, Madame Tussauds, London Zoo and the famous Abbey Road studios are all within a couple of miles of Lord's.

CELEBRITY WATCH: Paul McCartney liked the area so much while he recorded at Abbey Road he bought a house here. While on the subject of those who like legless people, war hero Douglas Bader was born in NW8. If one is perusing the coffee shops in St John's Wood High Street you may see Avram Grant, possibly doing some business with Kia Joorabchian, while Vanessa Feltz can be seen in the local cake shops. *Dragon's Den* star James Caan is another who lives locally, and cricket loving musicians Keith Richards and Lily Allen also reside here. With Nigel Kennedy, Mel Smith, Sachin Tendulkar and a host of others being around, St John's Wood is an autograph hunter's paradise!

NORTHAMPTONSHIRE

Northamptonshire County Cricket Club
The County Ground
Abington Avenue
Northampton
NN1 4PR

Club Colours: Maroon

Northamptonshire may never have won the County Championship, finishing second in 1957, '65 and '76, but the people in this region are just as passionate about their cricket as they are in any other part of the country. With some fine players in bygone years such as Allan and Tim Lamb, Colin Milburn, Ned Larkins, Peter Willey, David Capel and not forgetting the bank clerk who went to war, David Steele, the County Ground has seen some decent players over the years. When you throw in some of the overseas bunch such as Matthew Hayden, Kapil Dev, Dennis Lillee, Mike Hussey, Sarfraz Nawaz, Curtly Ambrose and Bishen Bedi, the list becomes even more impressive. So why have they never won the title? Financial reasons have often been a problem here, although now they are sorted. The side of the late 1950s, including Frank Tyson and Keith Andrew, were known as one of the best in the land, but on the other hand, Northants also hold the record for the longest sequence without a win, going for four years between May 1935 and May 1939 without recording a victory, a full 99 games! The folk of Northants must have been the only ones in the country pleased to see the Second World War. In recent years, the County Ground has been known as a Bunsen, but they have lost Swann and Panesar, their main protagonists with the spinning ball, and rely heavily on paceman Jack Brooks among a host of other youngsters. The future remains unclear for Northants, and quite frankly, the people of the third largest town not to be a city in the UK deserve better.

GROUNDS: Just purely Northampton now. The club did play fixtures in the past as far afield as Peterborough, Tring and Luton, along with Wellingborough and Stowe but now just tend to use Northampton. The ground has had quite a bit of work done in recent years, since the footballers moved out in 1994 and is a pleasant but not exciting enclosure. Always a decent track, it has tended to favour spin. The locals can make a decent atmosphere when sniffing success, but this has been thin on the ground in recent years. Not much singing has happened here, although Elton John did play live in June 2011.

TMS ANECDOTES: Ned Larkins is a hero to us at The Middle Stump. He was once offered a sponsorship deal with a local brewery of a pint a run, and needing no further incentive, picking up over 1,000 pints at the end of the 1980 season. A supposed poor influence on a young Phil Tufnell during a Caribbean tour, he was known to have had an abcess lanced with nothing more than a large scotch once in a remote place. Allan Lamb once quoted, 'If it was about drinking beer, Wayne Larkins would have been in the England team for years.' A true legend.

BANTER FACTOR: Jack Brooks, although he has unfortunately moved to Yorkshire. He bowls in a headband, likes a word or three and celebrates wickets with gusto! The Oxon oxen is a workhorse and will bowl all day, and can work up quite a head of steam. Brooks also tells us that Andrew Hall has a 'special bat' used for taking frustrations of a low score out in the dressing room, just so he doesn't smash up his main one!

BOOZERS: The Abington is quite nice these days now the football boys are over on the other side of town and regularly has guest ales, along with many local Northamptonshire ones. The Black Lion near the station is also worth a visit. Avoid the one the other side of the station, by the bridge towards the rugby ground on the edge of the estate! That is, unless you'd like a fight.

LOCAL BREW: Now we're talking. There are some fantastic local ales in this part of the world and Great Oakley's Wot's Occurring, along with golden ale Marching In, is very popular with the shoemaking folk in this region. Watch out for Tailshaker, their strong one, and their Gobble, described as giving a great feeling in the mouth, needs no further description in an upmarket publication such as this! The Frog Island beers and Hoggleys are worth a go, too. Nobby's Biggus Dickus would be very popular with the likes of Patrick Patterson or John Emburey.

OVERNIGHT STAY FACTOR: 1/10. Just far enough away from London to be a pain, while not really in the heart of the Midlands either, a stay in Northampton isn't many people's idea of a dream weekend away. Also beware if you do decide to stop, make sure that your visit doesn't coincide with the British Grand Prix at nearby Silverstone, when prices are known to go through the roof.

CELEBRITY WATCH: The only decent-looking Member of Parliament, Louise Mensch, represents nearby Corby, while rugby boys Courtney Lawes and Ben Cohen can still be spotted around town. Effeminate disc jockey Toby Anstis hails from these parts, as does the more masculine Jo Whiley. For those of a certain generation, Nanette Newman will more than happily get her Fairy Liquid out for you.

NOTTINGHAMSHIRE

Nottinghamshire County Cricket Club
Trent Bridge
Nottingham
NG2 6AG

Club Colours: Green and Yellow

One of the most decorated counties in the history of the game, Notts have won seventeen titles if you include their shared ones. One of their most famous players was George Gunn, him of Gunn & Moore family fame, a batmaker still based in Nottingham. Harold Larwood was another, but the post-war years were lean for this famous county until the arrival of Sir Garfield Sobers in the 1960s. Derek Randall, their most charismatic player, led them to a County Championship title in 1981, helped by the all-round brilliance of the South African Clive Rice and Kiwi Richard Hadlee. These two said their farewells to Trent Bridge in 1987 as they won the double of the County Championship and the NatWest trophy, and during this period they were always one of the strongest sides around. Now tending to generate their players from other counties, there is no doubt that with youngsters Alex Hales and James Taylor with the bat, and Luke Fletcher and Harry Gurney with the ball, the Outlaws will be one of the strongest sides in the years to come.

GROUNDS: Trent Bridge and Worksop. Trent Bridge is the third oldest test ground in the country, now fully equipped for the twenty-first century without losing its charm. Saying that, England have their poorest record here in the Ashes, with less than 15 per cent of wins gained. With the Radcliffe Road cricket centre costing £7.2 million and new stands at Fox Road and the Parr Stand opened by Prince Philip, a man renowned for his banter, it retains character aside from the tower block in the corner. Actually based in West Bridgford, walk out of the city centre, past Meadow Lane, home of Notts County and cross Trent Bridge itself. You'll see the Forest ground sitting aside the Trent, before you hit Trent Bridge cricket ground and its healthy 17,000 capacity. You get a great atmosphere here and on our last visit, a friend of The Middle Stump proceeded to down a bottle of Pimms before depositing it all over the Radcliffe Road a few hours later.

TMS ANECDOTES: Having played a bad-tempered game in 1930 at Southampton versus Hampshire, Bill Voce refused to stay on the field for the extra one run the home side needed and made them return the following day. The next morning his side turned up in lounge suits for the two balls needed to complete the match. Also on our last visit here we met a gentleman in the ground who told me that when he met his wife, she told him she suffered from chest pains, in fact she had acute angina. He replied, 'Aye, and your tits ain't too bad either!'

BANTER FACTOR: Graeme Swann. Rarely plays for the county these days due to his international commitments, and driving around to purchase screwdrivers in case his cats find themselves trapped under his floorboards.

BOOZERS: By the ground you have the Larwood and Voce tavern, which has plenty of West Bridgford yummy mummies around on non-match days. Head into town and plenty of the modern-day Maid Marians will serve you in Hooter's, while Ken Dodd always liked to pop into the

Vat & Fiddle on his visits. Carlton Street, Lace Market and the city centre all abound with pubs including the oldest in England, Ye Olde Trip to Jerusalem. However, my favourite is the Castle, situated next to, errr, the castle, which has been known to be the favoured watering hole of the England players on their visits to the Midlands. If any of the locals refer to you as 'mi duck' it is a term of endearment, and should no way be perceived as them taking the piss out of your batting average!

LOCAL BREW: Castle Rock, a local brewer, brought out Kiss Me Kate for the wedding of Prince William a couple of years back, and the Nottingham Brewery also provide some fine ales. Supreme at 5.2 per cent will make you fall over quicker than most, but my favourite has to be the fantastically named Cock and Hoop, served in the Cock and Hoop tavern!

OVERNIGHT STAY FACTOR: 8/10. Although not the prettiest of cities, Nottingham is an experience and is often combined with stag dos due to the men/women ratio that it is perceived to have. I like Nottingham; it has character, warmth and the people are good fun.

CELEBRITY WATCH: Nell Gwynn was given land here for sucking the pips out of Charles II's orange, while the antithesis of comedy also derives from these parts – the brilliant Richard Beckinsale and the not so brilliant Su Pollard and Leslie Crowther. Sporting heroes Torvill and Dean, Carl Froch and Stuart Broad can regularly be spotted, while David Pleat is known to drive his car slowly around the city – allegedly! For the cultured, Lord Byron hailed from here, while Sir Paul Smith will design you a suit if asked nicely. Former head of MI5 Stella Rimington is a Nottingham lass, while political bruisers Ken Clarke and Ed Balls can often be seen squaring up to each other after a night out in the Lace Market!

SOMERSET

Somerset County Cricket Club
The County Ground
Taunton
TA1 1JT

Club Colours: Black, White and Maroon

Unbelievably, the Cidermen have never won the County Championship. The county were always treated as a good fun side, inconsistent and had the element of being a good place to tour. That all changed in the 1970s with the arrival of Brian Close, the emergence of Sir Ian Botham (in the days before he was a Sir of course) and those two brilliant West Indians, another Sir, Vivian Richards, and the man they called Big Bird, Joel Garner. Amazingly, they only won their first trophy in 1979, when the Gillette Cup and the John Player League made their way west, but are now one of the best sides in the country. The 1980s was an era filled with controversy, with the sackings of the West Indian pair followed by that acrimonious meeting in Shepton Mallet. Botham resigned and went to Worcestershire and Martin Crowe arrived, with Peter Roebuck taking the captaincy mantle. A period in the silverware wilderness followed. Now a name on the world stage after a brave exit to the Mumbai Indians in the Champions League T20, the future is bright with the emergence of some extremely talented youngsters such as Buttler, Barrow, Gregory, Dockrell, Dibble, Waller and the Overtons. Allied to the experience of the world-class Trescothick, it is no wonder this is a county always among the turf accountants' favourites for any trophy.

GROUNDS: Taunton, Bath, Weston-super-Mare. Taunton is one of the prettiest grounds in the country with the church spires to the southern end, and the Quantock Hills to the north, giving it a beautiful natural setting. Although only holding 8,500 people, the atmosphere here when the cider is flowing can be fairly robust to say the least! It is our sort of ground here at The Middle Stump. You are bound to hear some fine banter coming from the crowd. The ground has undergone a major transformation in recent years and more is on the way, we understand.

Enter either by the JCW Gates in St James Street, or the Sir Viv Richards Gates in Priory Bridge Road. The museum here is also well worth a visit.

TMS ANECDOTES: Joel Garner, who was 6ft 8in tall, was once asked by an admirer down in Taunton whether he was all in proportion. Big Bird replied, 'Darling, if I was all in proportion I'd be 10ft 6in!'

BANTER FACTOR: Steve Kirby, one of the funniest men around. Also look out for the tattooed Peter Trego.

BOOZERS: The Cricketers between the station and the ground comes recommended by our sources, as does the Crown & Sceptre, who offer a fine selection of real ales, along with live music and a pool table. Try and find a pub with a skittle alley if you can. Skittles is a Somerset version of ten pin bowling and is the hub of a good night out. Please, though, boys and girls, try and behave as Taunton is the home to 40 Commando of the Royal Marines!

LOCAL BREW: No visit to the West would be complete without trying a scrumpy or some decent local cider such as Thatchers. They are obsessed with cider, and you can even get cider slush, a sort of iced slush puppy type drink to cool you down after a hot day on the combine harvester.

OVERNIGHT STAY FACTOR: 9/10. One of the prettiest parts of the country with the Quantocks, Exmoor and the Mendips all within a short drive, along with some of the most beautiful coastline in the UK. We'd definitely recommend an overnighter in this part of the world, especially if you could also combine your visit with a trip to Taunton races.

CELEBRITY WATCH: For those of a certain era, sexy actress Jenny Agutter was born in Taunton, while be careful getting out your guitar here as a local lady may marry you. Pattie Boyd, wife of George Harrison and Eric Clapton, hails from the town, as does former Scotland rugby coach, Andy Robinson. Phil Vickery, no not that one, the celebrity chef also resides in the town, and spiky haired know-it-all Gary Rhodes trained at the Castle Hotel here between 1986 and 1990.

SURREY

Surrey County Cricket Club
The Kia Oval
Kennington
London
SE11 5SS

Club Colours: Brown

Since the days of the Prince of Wales, the future Edward VIII, allowing Surrey to use the Prince of Wales' feathers as their emblem, the county has always had a reputation for being aristocratic. Although being based in one of the poorest areas of London, I really am not sure why? The pre-war years read like a Who's Who as Sir Jack Hobbs, Andy Sandham, Alf Gover, Douglas Jardine, and the wonderful Percy Fender all plied their trade at The Oval. Times were good after the Second World War, and in the 1950s Surrey were unstoppable. The Bedsers, Laker and Lock would bowl sides out before Peter May, Stuart Surridge and Kenny Barrington would get the runs. The '1970s and '80s were a drought by their standards, but the 1990s would provide the likes of Alec Stewart, Mark Butcher, Graham Thorpe, Martin Bicknell and Mark Ramprakash to the England team. Over the next few years, it remains to be seen whether youngsters Rory Hamilton-Brown, Jason Roy, Stuart Meaker, Jade Dernbach and the emerging Freddie van den Bergh can add to the Brown Hatters' nineteen County Championship titles. One thing this county isn't short of, however, is character.

GROUNDS: The Oval, Whitgift school in Croydon and Guildford. The 23,500-capacity Kia Oval was the first in England to hold an international, and is one of only two grounds to have football and cricket internationals played there, along with Bramall Lane in Sheffield. With Aussie Rules now being played there and potentially a hotel, the ground maximises its hemmed-in surroundings. Nice and close to Oval station, you turn left and you are outside the Pavilion End. No two ends in cricket are so different, with the history and ancient architecture of the pavilion at one end, while the Vauxhall End is now dominated by the modern OCS Stand. The famous gasometer is to the right of this stand as you look from the Pavilion End. I always used to like The Oval; you could get really pissed there without people looking down on you as they did sometimes at Lord's, but overzealous stewarding in recent years, when it has come to 'beer snakes' and the like, has ruined this impression.

TMS ANECDOTES: David Smith, the 'Balham bruiser', was a man with a fearsome reputation in the 1980s. He once offered me and about thirty of my friends a chance to continue our conversation behind the pavilion after a game once, after getting slightly loud in a NatWest game against Hertfordshire. Yes just him! He also got chatted out by Paul Nixon at Leicester once and the Leicester players were worried for Nico's safety, especially when Smith punched a hole in the dressing room door. After the game, the Leicester keeper came into the car park and Smith was there waiting. Preparing for death from the 6ft 3in South Londoner, Smith merely shook Nico's hand and told him he shouldn't have allowed him to get under his skin, to much relief from the Cumbrian stumper!

BANTER FACTOR: Steve Davies. After his brave decision to come out as gay, the ex-Worcestershire wicketkeeper no doubt still gets the odd comment in the macho world of county cricket. I'm sure he has a few comebacks in his repertoire to silence his critics. Irishman Gary Wilson also has plenty of amusing one-liners as well.

BOOZERS: For the cultural, the White Bear close to Kennington station serves a great pint and has fringe theatre upstairs. For the less cultured, unfortunately the Queen Anne at Vauxhall is now shut, as the young ladies there would let you admire their damp tracks and ovals, if you should put a pound in their pint glass! The Royal Vauxhall Tavern caters for the 'brown hatters' among the Brown Hatters as it is a gay bar, but my advice is head for Waterloo and the South Bank. For the up market you have venues such as Skylon, but we'd recommend the Kings Arms in Roupell Street which is two minutes' walk from Waterloo. Great beers, Thai food served and a top beer garden. The other one we like is the Young's pub, the Founders Arms with the Thames lapping the shore next to you. Amazing views abound from here and there is plenty of life, along with great beer. Studio Six in nearby Gabriel's Wharf is also decent with many lagers from around the world.

LOCAL BREW: Beefeater Gin is still distilled in Montford Place in Kennington, don't you know. Sambrooks is a microbrewery in nearby Battersea which produces Wandle, named after the river, and Junction, presumably named after Clapham's train station! Young's at Wandsworth was Britain's oldest brewery.

OVERNIGHT STAY FACTOR: 9/10. If it was Kennington and the locality I would give it a 1/10 but head to the South Bank, an area always known for entertainment. From the days of Shakespeare, it was known for 'theatres, prostitutes and bear baiting' and the Globe is based here. With County Hall, the London Eye, Tate Modern, Oxo Tower and National Theatre all here, it is a great place to hang out with the in crowd.

CELEBRITY WATCH: Always known for spotting an MP, as Kennington was described as the place where they all own their second homes. In the art world, Hogarth and Van Gogh lived here for a while, while Charlie Chaplin also resided in this part of South London. Kevin Spacey has been known to 'walk his dog' here occasionally in the early hours of the morning when not directing at the nearby Old Vic, while ex-gangster now turned celebrity Mad Frankie Fraser was known to remove people's teeth with pliers around SE11.

SUSSEX

Sussex County Cricket Ground
Eaton Road
Hove
East Sussex
BN3 3AN

Club Colours: Blue and White

The oldest county in England and home to where the game of cricket began on the South Downs, although both Kent and Hampshire also lay claim to this fame. For the first 164 years of their existence, County Championships were spotted as many times as a real-life martlet, the mythological footless bird on the Sussex badge, in this part of the world. Then like London buses, they all flocked here at once after they broke their duck in 2003, with trophies following in 2006 and 2007. In fact, with ten trophies in ten years at the start of the millennium, you could say Sussex are the most successful county of the twenty-first century. Some fine players have graced this club, such as John Wisden and the prince, Ranji. In the 1970s both Tony Grieg and John Snow would let the coastal breeze blow through their locks, and there have been some outstanding overseas Pakistanis. Javed Miandad and Imran Khan both had long stints at Hove, and Mushtaq Ahmed, with his three-striped Adidas beard, spun them to the title before taking on the role as spin coach to the England team. With 10 million quid left to them by a rather generous supporter

a few years ago, it remains to be seen whether youngsters such as Joe Gatting, Will Beer, Luke Wells and Ben Brown can continue the fine traditions of this South Coast club.

GROUNDS: Hove, the stunning Arundel, Eastbourne, Horsham, and it is a bloody shame the old ground at Hastings is now a supermarket! Hove is a traditional venue, one where you can still smell the sea and has blue and white deckchairs to watch the game from. The flats still overlook the ground, but the old bus shelter known as the Arthur Gilligan Stand is no longer. Unusually square in shape, beware after buying your food at the excellent Sid's Snack Shack that the local seagulls don't dive-bomb you. Loads of work has been done in recent years to this venue, with the new Farnrise Indoor Cricket school. Situated just an Ian Grieg long hop away from Hove station, enter via the Tate gates on Eaton Road, or the North East gate on Palmeira Avenue. The only other word of warning is that a lot of the best seats are taken up by members or corporate seating. Other than that, grounds like this have immense character, but be prepared to wrap up warm at times.

TMS ANECDOTES: Jim Parks, the senior one not his son who also played, scored a mere 3,003 runs and took 101 wickets back in 1937. His reward was to be selected for the England team, sharing his debut with Len Hutton. After scoring 22 and 7, he was promptly dropped and never played for England again!

BANTER FACTOR: Sussex have had many characters in recent years, notably Ed Giddins, Martin Speight and Dermot Reeve, but the current banter man is Matt Prior. The darling of the North London glaziers after smashing the windows at Lord's, Prior tried to blame the incident on a glove! Still, it sounds more feasible than Ricky Ponting who tried to blame a hole in a television once, on a box he had thrown. Others to have smashed property are Mark Ramprakash who demolished Adam Hollioake's helmet once after a warning about keeping his temper, Mike Atherton who broke a toe kicking a table, and Nasser Hussain who totalled a fridge once in Pakistan, after a dubious lbw decision.

BOOZERS: Whatever your creed, colour or religion, Hove and neighbouring Brighton will have something for you. We recommend the Cricketers, just a Luke Wright six hit away, and a boozer where you can actually see the scoreboard. Cask Ales abound here, as do different guest ales, although it can get busy. The Blind Busker is also recommended, and on a Monday they do a superb music quiz, with top banter from the compère apparently. The Hove Place is expensive but do a lamb shank to die for, you know where the meat just falls off of the bone? A short walk away in Brighton, there are loads. And I do mean loads. As a man who has toured in this part of the world, I'm an expert.

LOCAL BREW: With over thirty independent breweries in Sussex alone, not even Oliver Reed and Richard Burton could drink this place dry. Southdowns' Rankins Ram at 4 per cent is good, but the Devil's Dyke Porter at 5 per cent will want to make you sleep on the stony beach. Harvey's is another good brewery based in nearby Lewes, using water from the River Ouse.

OVERNIGHT STAY FACTOR: 8/10. Nightlife abounds in this place, but for those of a quieter nature, the nearby Sussex Downs offer tranquillity and beauty. Don't think you have sniffed the poppers too much if you see something that looks the Taj Mahal in the centre of Brighton. This is the Royal Pavilion and has some outstanding architecture. The Lanes, with their intimate alleyways and antique shops are worth a visit. Other alleyways such as those from the first brilliant gangster chic film, Graham Greene's *Brighton Rock* can be seen, as can the one that saw Leslie Ash getting hammered like a Tony Pigott over in *Quadrophenia*.

CELEBRITY WATCH: A real haunt of the rich and famous, Steve Ovett lives here. Don't do the opposite of what one bloke did to his arch nemesis Seb Coe, and thinking he was Ovett, went up to him and said, 'I loved it when you pissed all over that smug wanker, Seb Coe,' when in fact he was talking to the man behind our Olympic bid himself! On no account also take the pith out of local man Chwith Eubank, while Fatboy Slim can often be seen around town with Zoe Ball. Peter Andre can often be seen flexing his six pack, and Des Lynam is still the oldest smoothie in Kemp Town. Newsreader Carol Barnes is from these parts, while the boyfriends of Holly Willoughby and Jordan aka Katie Price have been known to have admired a damp track at Hove.

WARWICKSHIRE

Edgbaston
Edgbaston Road
Birmingham
West Midlands
B5 7QU

Club Colours: Black and Gold

Founded in Leamington Spa in 1882, Warwickshire weren't much good frankly, until the two Franks, Field and Foster, bowled them to the title in 1911 with a mere 238 wickets between them. After the Second World War, Eric Hollies bowled them to the title in 1946, while in the 1950s, M.J.K. Smith and Tom Cartwright were the main men in Britain's second city. The early 1970s brought success and the likes of Dennis Amiss, Lance Gibbs, Rohan Kanhai and Alvin Kallicharan were heroes in Birmingham. The next twenty years were as awful as the acting in *Crossroads*, the soap set in a Birmingham motel, and Bob Willis was Benny, brilliant for England but not so for the Bears. The 1990s, however, brought huge success and the treble of 1994 under Bob Woolmer and Dermot Reeve included the highest ever score in the game's history, the 501 not out by Brian Lara. The 810–4 they amassed was also a record against Durham that day. They followed this up with a double the following year, but then the next few years were a bit frugal and some infighting, leading to the sacking of Kiwi coach Mark Greatbatch, occurred. Now under Ashley Giles, they have a great team with Rikki Clarke their talisman, as well as England batsmen Jonathan Trott and Ian Bell, and they were champions in 2012. The young players they have coming through mean that the Bears will be strong for the next few years as the likes of Laurie Evans, Richard Johnson, Keith Barker, Steffan Piolet and Chris Woakes make their mark.

GROUNDS: Edgbaston. Have been known to visit Coventry and Leamington Spa but Edgbaston is where the home is. The second-best ground in the country behind Lord's, Alec Stewart described it 'as partisan as Eden Gardens in Calcutta' and it can get lively here when full, especially in the Eric Hollies Stand, or what was the old Rea Bank.

This stand holds 6,000 and when the Brummies have had a few sherbets, this place rocks – especially during England games. Based just south of the city centre, Edgbaston held the first day/night game in the UK and has had £32 million spent on the south side of the ground alone in recent years! The many stands include the South, which has a great visitor and learning centre, and the West, which is a two-tiered affair and houses the Edgbaston suite. In the Bob Wyatt Stand there are a couple of restaurants and a museum, while the press stand is alcohol free. Never more have I heard of such a misnomer for a stand! Chuck in the Raglan, the Priory, the small one by the scorebox and the Eric Hollies, and it really is a twenty-first-century venue these days, but without losing the atmosphere it has always had. No wonder it is such a stronghold for England, and with 25,000 in it, it seriously makes some noise.

TMS ANECDOTEs: Eddie Hemmings was a legend in these parts before his move to Nottingham and was once walking along the road after a Test match in Australia, having not played, along with fellow Bear, Gladstone Small. Hemmings was collared by an ex-pat who was asking him all sorts of questions such as, 'What's Birmingham like these days?', and, 'Who is coming through at Edgbaston?' This guy hadn't been in the UK for ten years or so, and the conversation came round to Gladstone. The ex-pat asked Hemmings what he was like, and Eddie pointed to his partner and said that this was indeed Gladstone and would he like to meet him. The bloke took one look at the hunchback walking alongside him and said in the broadest Brummie accent, 'Well there's no need to take the piss Eddie, I was only trying to be nice,' before walking off!

BANTER FACTOR: Rikki Clarke, an absolute legend and good friend of us here at The Middle Stump. In fact, all of the Warwickshire lads like our work, and often comment on what we do. Rikki was made captain of the Ugly XI before responding that Dan could be twelfth man, and he is trialling a couple of new players. When asked who they were, he replied with his mum and dad!

BOOZERS: In the city centre there are thousands. More locally, the Plough in Harborne has local ales, good wine, a large beer garden and handmade pizzas on offer, that great Brummie fayre! The Garden House offers good food too, with their steaks and fish being of good quality, while the White Swan and the Gun Barrels in Bristol Road also pass The Middle Stump test. The City Tavern in Five Ways is another, but literally there are loads and loads.

LOCAL BREW: Rather disappointingly, Birmingham's pubs are dominated by the big chains like Punch and Enterprise but there are a couple of smaller ones. Burton on Trent and all of its brewing is not far, but we recommend the Highgate Brewery from Walsall and their Dark Mild or the Davenport range. Also there is a Warwickshire Beer Company who brew the famous Churchyard Bob. Named after Willis?

OVERNIGHT STAY FACTOR: 3/10. While the broken windows of Fort Dunlop don't look out over the M6 anymore, and Birmingham has more canals than Venice, a weekend in Britain's second city isn't exactly on everyone's list of romantic breaks. Unless you are staying for one of the numerous events at the NEC, the tennis in Edgbaston or a spell in rehab at the Priory, forget it.

CELEBRITY WATCH: Neville Chamberlain was the most famous man to pull out a piece of paper from these parts, until Denesh Ramdin did it at Edgbaston in 2012. J.R.R. Tolkien wrote *The Hobbit* about Ian Bell, while Nick Mason of Pink Floyd also came from here. As for Birmingham, then the Cat who got the cream, Miss Deeley is from here, as is Ozzy Osbourne. On the far right, Ron Atkinson and Enoch Powell are/were Brummies as was another Powell known to talk nonsense, Radio 1 DJ Peter. You may see Martin Shaw wandering around, while musically this is the place that has given the world Toyah and Musical Youth. Better stuff came back in the day from Joan Armatrading and UB40, while The Streets' Mike Skinner left the beauty of Barnet where I am from, to settle here. He must be mad! Bring your autograph books, as with the Priory being in Edgbaston, this is a hive of celebrities.

WORCESTERSHIRE

The County Ground
New Road
Worcester
Worcs
WR2 4QQ

Club Colours: Dark Green, Black and White

Formed in 1899, Worcester were extremely weak in their early existence and almost went out of the championship. In 1919 they couldn't raise a side and in 1920, they were caned more times than Frank Bough, losing three times by an innings and 200 runs. Their fortunes turned when they recruited the Nawab of Pataudi in the 1930s, but it was the 1960s with Norman Gifford, Tom Graveney and the wonderful Basil D'Oliveira that brought home the title for the Pears. The 1970s brought the Kiwi Glenn Turner to New Road, who scored a shed load, while in the 1980s they became the Man United of cricket, attracting the best players from other counties. Ian Botham and Graham Dilley came here and with the Zimbabwean Graeme Hick, they were the best side in the country, thanks to the influence of local batmaker, Duncan Fearnley. A side that has been up and down like a whore's knickers recently, it remains to be seen if the likes of Kervezee, Moeen Ali and Jack Shantry can return those glory years back for them, along with the third generation in the famous D'Oliveira dynasty, Brett.

GROUNDS: Possibly the most picturesque ground on the circuit is New Road, but they also play at Kidderminster and Stourbridge occasionally.

New Road is an amazing venue, and although merely holding 4,500 and being prone to flooding from the nearby River Severn, there is something magical about it. Overshadowed by the cathedral, the ground is a mishmash of small enclosures and the Ladies' Pavilion is something out of history. Described by Graeme Fowler as a 'proper sort of place, where you are served by lovely women with the pinnies on,' the cake there is homemade and extremely popular. It is sold off at just a pound a slice and Mike Selvey tells us, 'it would be churlish not to'. From Shrub Hill or Foregate Street stations head for the river and the huge cathedral, cross the Severn and it is on your left after the bridge.

TMS ANECDOTES: Adrian Shankar was a batsman who Worcestershire sacked from his contract in 2011 due to fraudulent claims on his CV. Not only did this Billy Bullshitter lie about his past credentials, claiming he had played a better standard than he actually had, he also lied about his age as well, meaning the Pears were in trouble with the ECB about the under-26-year-old's payments. He claimed to have played tennis at National Level and football for Arsenal as well. Having been released from Lancashire a couple of years previously, Luke Sutton allegedly pulled him up about his age of which he just claimed that he had spent his first three years on a life support machine, and therefore it was not applicable! I wonder where he is now?

BANTER FACTOR: Norman Gifford was a legend at Worcester but would throw some awful tantrums. Once after his side were bowled all out for a low score at Lord's, they were feasting on the lunches served there. Giff removed all the food as a form of punishment and sent them away to the nets in the Nursery End.

BOOZERS: The city centre is an alcoholic's wet dream with the amount of hostelries, but if you stay the New Road side of the river, then the Wheatsheaf on Hylton Road by the university comes highly recommended. Offering six real ales, it has views over the river and the city centre and is a top venue. The Cricketers on Angel Street is another good place, with memorabilia all over the walls of cricket in general with lots of cigarette cards, photos and the like. Near to Foregate Street station the Dragon Inn and the Saracens Head are both decent, but there are literally loads here to take your pick from.

LOCAL BREW: Cannon Royall is a local brewery that comes highly recommended but we are going to plump for Hobsons with their fine range of ales. Best at 3.8 per cent and Town Crier at 4.5 per cent are both popular, but Old Henry at 5.2 per cent is what the hardcore Pears fans drink.

OVERNIGHT STAY FACTOR: 9/10. With its floodlit cathedral and Tudor architecture, not built by Alex, Worcester is a wonderful city to stay in and one which we recommend highly. In this land of hope and glory visit Elgar's birthplace, attend the factory where Lea & Perrins make their Worcester sauce or see where Cromwell's New Model Army beat the Cavaliers. Further south on the River Severn you can see the Severn Bore at certain times. This isn't one of the old blokes in the pavilion who sits and does the scoring of county games, with his headphones on. It is a tidal wave that goes the wrong way back up the river, and can be surfed.

CELEBRITY WATCH: Worcester isn't exactly throbbing with celebrities it has to be said! Beverly Hills it ain't. One of the most famous was Hannah Snell, a crossdresser who managed to become one of our best ever soldiers by lying about her gender. I've seen her portrait and you would need quite a few Old Henry's if you know what I mean! Fay Weldon will write about Worcester, while our most famous composer with a grand total of two symphonies, Edward Elgar, also hailed from here. Throw in DJ Priceless, Rik Mayall, the darling of the Worcestershire players, Cher Lloyd, and finally the cricketer who has confused dyslexics since the 1960s, Brian Brain.

YORKSHIRE

Headingley Carnegie Cricket Ground
Leeds
LS6 3BU

Club Colours: Dark Blue, Light Blue and Gold

Cricket is like a religion in Yorkshire and Headingley is the church they come to pray at, while apostles like Boycott and Trueman are remembered fondly. Cricket has been played since 1751 with the game forming around Sheffield, but it wasn't until a century later that things started to get organised and they started to play at Bramall Lane, now home of Sheffield United. Fourteen years later they had the first of many rows which have scarred this county, with five players refusing to play. Lord Hawke and Wilfred Rhodes were the main men for the White Rose county at the start of the twentieth century, and between the wars the likes of Herbert Sutcliffe, Hedley Verity and Len Hutton meant that they were without a doubt, the best side in the country for many years. If England needed a quickie, they would whistle down the local pit and a fast bowler would emerge, so the saying went. After the war, the 1950s saw the emergence of Freddie Trueman, Brian Close and Bob Appleyard, and they returned to dominance in the 1960s as the likes of Close, Ray Illingworth, Geoff Boycott and John Hampshire made their mark. Close was sacked in 1970 and when Boycott was sacked in 1978 there was almost civil war! In 1992 their Yorkshire-born players policy was abandoned, meaning the likes of Michael Vaughan and Sachin Tendulkar could play, and the title came back to Leeds in 2001 under David Byas. Now under the shrewd coaching of Jason Gillespie, it is down to the youngsters such as Joe Root, Jonny Bairstow and Moin Ashraf to see if they can add to their thirty-one County Championship titles, the best of any side bar none. 2013 sees them return to the top division.

GROUNDS: Headingley and Scarborough. Scarborough is a great place when the sun shines but we are going to concentrate on Headingley, which has changed beyond belief in the last ten years. Two miles to the north-west of Leeds city centre, get a train to Headingley and turn left into Kirkstall Lane. You can't miss the new Carnegie Pavilion in front of you, which has replaced the old Winter Sheds, and now houses the media centre. This £21 million structure dominates the ground and although described as being like 'Gaudi, when he were pissed', I quite like it and think it adds character to the venue. Upstairs are new offices, banqueting suites and executive boxes while at pitch level you have the Trueman Enclosure. To the left are the North East and Family stands which are alcohol free, followed by the new East Stand. The Main Stand further round still backs on to the rugby league ground. Completing the bowl effect, you have the open Western Stand, once home of some outrageous behaviour but good fun all the same. Plans are in place to introduce a museum and this ground is completely different to the one where we beat the Aussies in '81, the scene of one of England's finest victories. A true Test venue, and one of which all Yorkshiremen should be proud.

TMS ANECDOTEs: Four Yorkshire captains have either won or retained the Ashes for England, yet ironically none were skipper of Yorkshire at the time. Stanley Jackson, Len Hutton and Michael Vaughan all played for the White Rose, while Ray Illingworth was in exile at Leicestershire at the time. Strange but true.

BANTER FACTOR: Anthony McGrath is supposedly one of the funniest men around on the circuit and is quick to come back with a one-liner or two. Coach Jason Gillespie is another, and he even has a wine named in honour of his double century as a night watchman, Dizzy 201.

BOOZERS: Headingley is student land, and there are pubs aplenty. The Otley Road is the place to go where you can take your pick. The Box is OK, albeit a bit young, as is the Original Oak. The Skyrack can be known for trouble and the locals joke it sells plasma on draught! My sources advise the Three Horseshoes with a good mix of locals and students and good cask beer. Watch out if there is something called the Otley Run taking place. This is where the students dress up in fancy dress and go on a huge pub crawl. It can make things busy, and pisses off the locals no end, while these posh kids from Surrey think they are the most original people ever for doing this.

LOCAL BREW: Now we are talking! Joshua Tetley founded the Tetley Brewery in Leeds in 1822, although Smoothflow is the only beer still produced in the county. The rest have been sold off and are now made in Northampton and Hartlepool. John Smith's is still based at Tadcaster, and Timothy Taylor and their famous Landlord is from nearby Keighley. We recommend the Black Sheep from North Yorkshire though and Black Sheep Ale at 4.4 per cent is decent, as is a blond beer they do called Golden Sheep. Riggwelter at 5.9 per cent sorts out the shandy-drinking cockney students up there on a regular basis!

OVERNIGHT STAY FACTOR: 7/10. 'Don't talk to me about culture, ah've been to Leeds,' said Harry Enfield's famous Yorkshireman, George Integrity Whitebread. Leeds as a city has affluence in the centre, yet some of the most deprived areas in the UK in other parts. It has become one of the main commercial centres, especially in finance and law. The Briggate offers great shopping and Trinity Leeds is due to open soon. Clarence Dock offers a marina of bars and restaurants but I'd use this as a base to see some of the great countryside this world offers. Brontë Country, home of *Wuthering Heights* and Heathcliff, not Heath Streak is nearby, as are the Dales and further afield the city of York and the North Yorkshire Moors. Well worth a visit.

CELEBRITY WATCH: Playwrights Alan Bennett and Helen Fielding of Bridget Jones fame hail from Leeds, as does Jeremy Dyson, writer of the *League of Gentlemen*. Loudmouths Jeremy Paxman, Alex Zane and Chris Moyles are from here, while the face of John Craven is still scaring kids to this day, as does Mel B. Better-looking Nell McAndrew and Gabby Logan brighten up the scene, while the Kaiser Chiefs can be spotted in the city centre, predicting a riot. The ghost of Ernie Wise is known to haunt the place, while The Middle Stump friend and tweeter Fred Boycott is known to dig in around the Headingley area.

Visit our website and discover thousands of other History Press books.

www.thehistorypress.co.uk

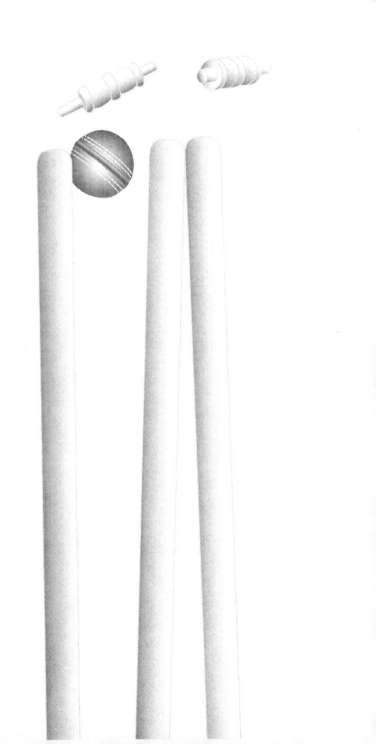

Lightning Source UK Ltd.
Milton Keynes UK
UKOW04f0719050814

236370UK00001B/1/P